THE
DEVIL
EMAILS AT
MIDNIGHT

FROM *WALL STREET JOURNAL* AND *USA TODAY* BEST-SELLING AUTHOR

MITA MALLICK

THE DEVIL EMAILS AT MIDNIGHT

WHAT GOOD LEADERS CAN LEARN FROM BAD BOSSES

WILEY

Published by John Wiley & Sons, Inc., Hoboken, New Jersey.
Published simultaneously in Canada.

The manufacturer's authorized representative according to the EU General Product Safety Regulation is Wiley-VCH GmbH, Boschstr. 12, 69469 Weinheim, Germany, e-mail: Product_Safety@wiley.com.

For general information on our other products and services or for technical support, please contact our Customer Care Department within the United States at (800) 762-2974, outside the United States at (317) 572-3993 or fax (317) 572-4002.

Wiley also publishes its books in a variety of electronic formats. Some content that appears in print may not be available in electronic formats. For more information about Wiley products, visit our web site at www.wiley.com.

Library of Congress Cataloging-in-Publication Data is Available:

ISBN 9781394316489 (Cloth)
ISBN 9781394316496 (ePub)
ISBN 9781394316502 (ePDF)

Cover Design: Wiley
Cover Images: © coolvectormaker/Getty Images and Wiley
Author Photo: © JWJ Photography
Printed and bound by CPI Group (UK) Ltd, Croydon, CR0 4YY

C9781394316489_280925

For Jay and Priya:

Even though I am a writer, I can't quite find the words to express how much I love you both.

And someday, when you come to me and your father to complain about your bad boss, I will hand you this book.

Contents

Introduction

I have been a bad boss.

And chances are, so have you.

Over the years, I have thought about my bad boss phases. Do my colleagues still remember me as a bad boss? Did they have clever nicknames they still use for me if ever they think of me?

Was I known as Maleficent?

Perhaps I was a bit cold and aloof when I first started managing teams because you aren't supposed to be friends with your direct reports. And right, I also went through my wearing only black phase to project that I was a boss to be taken very seriously. Especially in the beauty industry.

Or micromanaging Mita?

In all fairness, I was only particular about the important details. The images on slides, the title of the slides, the content on the slides, the back-up/appendix/cover-our-a$$ slides, and of course the talk track for the actual presentation. And then the dress rehearsal for the presentation before the actual presentation.

How about Medusa?

That seems a bit harsh, doesn't it? People weren't ever scared to present to me and look me directly in the eyes, were they? How could I have the power to frighten someone so badly they would be unable to speak or interact with me or others?

1

Over the course of my own career, I have always been quick to cleverly name some of my bad bosses. I would paint them as a Disney villain or an evil Marvel character or a scary witch from a childhood fairytale or other mythical, magical characters or powerful objects. Even my mother would know their nicknames, asking me over FaceTime *"How's the Dragon Lady doing today?"* after I had endured another long and torturous day of work.

My having nicknames for my bad bosses maybe was a way to cope with my attempts—and sometimes very long journey—to survive that bad boss. And, maybe as a way to separate myself from them and create some much-needed emotional distance. Because I could never be as bad of a boss as they were.

Could I?

Because I had worked for some of the "baddest" of the bad bosses. The bad boss who fell asleep in meetings. The bad boss who took credit for all my work, and I mean *all* of it. The bad boss who once threw her designer shoe at my colleague. (I was able to dodge that Chanel heel and it thankfully missed my colleague's head, too.) The bad boss who told me I was a rat and demanded loyalty. The bad boss who told me I was overconfident and needed to stay in my lane. The bad boss who gossiped about me to others and told my peers I didn't really know what I was doing. The bad boss who was so nice and so profoundly incompetent, that as much as I wanted to, it was really hard to hate him.

And here's the thing I have come to discover about bad bosses. Bad bosses aren't born bad. Bad bosses are made. They are a product of their circumstances.

Some bad bosses have never been trained to lead. They are just promoted and promoted and promoted because they are great individual contributors. They have great expertise. And no one ever told them that they were now in charge of other people's careers.

Some bad bosses are deeply wounded. They say hurt people hurt people. They enjoy lashing out at others, taunting and teasing, shouting in private and in public, humiliating their team members. It can provide them a sense of temporary relief while at the same time solidifying their power.

Some bad bosses only ever worked for other bad bosses. They just model the bad behavior they witnessed and think that's the way to lead. They pick up terrible habits and never unlearn the things they aren't supposed to do at work. (Or at home, for that matter.)

Some bad bosses don't have the expertise to do their jobs. They managed to successfully keep failing up. They don't know how to set strategy, give direction, when to start, stop, or continue the work. Sometimes they are incompetent and mean, which makes them easier to detest. When they are incompetent and nice, well, that makes things a bit more complicated.

Some bad bosses can't operate without micromanaging every single little detail. Sometimes they don't know what they are supposed to be doing, so they do your job for you. Sometimes they don't trust you to do your job, so they do your job for you. Sometimes they control all of the details at work and do your job because they are feeling a loss of control of their lives outside of their work.

Some bad bosses are temporarily bad. They have been passed up for a promotion, again. Or they are being horribly bullied by their own bad boss. Or they don't have much power or influence or respect of their peers at work. Or their entire identity and sense of self-worth is tied to this one job. Or they are overworked and under-resourced. Or they have no idea what to do next because their own boss can't make any decisions. Or they have lost someone they love, and they are struggling with grief.

I have experienced each and every one of those situations as the boss, and I know I am not alone. Once upon a time, I too was that bad boss. And since those bad boss moments, I have been on a journey to avoid being the bad boss. To truly understand and accept that my behavior can negatively or positively affect someone else's experience at work and affect their overall lives and well-being.

I once read on LinkedIn that your boss can have the most significant impact on your mental health. More than your spouse or partner. More than your parents. More than your children. More than your best friend. So, imagine the difference between a bad boss and a good leader. Imagine the difference a bad boss versus a good leader can have on our workplaces. Some of you don't have to imagine it; you have lived it. You have survived the bad boss to get to the other side of what it feels like to be appreciated, valued, recognized, and seen in our workplaces. To work with people who don't just tolerate you (or worse, harm you) but they celebrate you. They elevate you. They lift you up. They cheer you on. They coach you through mistakes. Because that's what good bosses do. And that's when bosses no longer are bosses. They become good leaders. Some even go on to be great.

In my first book, *Reimagine Inclusion: Debunking 13 Myths to Transform Your Workplace,* I talked about why inclusion matters so much in our workplaces. Many of us go to work to collect our paychecks and pay our bills. Some of us also enjoy what we do and are building our careers on our expertise, and helping others build their careers, too. And we spend more time at work than in our homes and in our communities. In fact, the average person will spend one-third of their life at work, about 90,000 hours.[1] We spend too much time at work not to be included.

And what does inclusion in the workplace even mean?

When I am included at work, I know my work is valued. My voice, my contributions, my expertise—all of it matters. I am recognized for what I do on my team and in my organization, and people see me. I have the ability to reach my potential and my company can then reach its potential. Because I feel included, I will go above and beyond without being asked to do so.

And the individual who can have the biggest impact on whether or not we feel included in our workplaces?

Our boss.

Simply put, because the boss holds enormous power in our organizations, whether we like it or not, whether or not they have earned it or deserve it. And our bosses aren't the only ones with authority in our lives who can make us feel excluded, like we don't belong, like we don't matter.

Consider the following scenarios. Have you ever experienced these particular situations, or can you imagine experiencing them with individuals with some type of authority? How would it make you feel?

- When the teacher never calls on you when you raise your hand
- When the police officer doesn't believe you were robbed
- When the coach keeps you benched despite your talent
- When the host of the party who invited you ignores you
- When the doctor dismisses your symptoms

Just like these scenarios, bad bosses can also illicit very similar feelings for us. Because this is what most bad bosses have in common:

- They don't see us.
- They invalidate our experiences.
- They dismiss, minimize, or worse, try to chip away at us.
- They don't see our value or our worth.
- They can make us feel like what we do at work doesn't matter.

And that ultimately makes us feel that we don't matter to them or the organization.

A bad boss can break inclusion. A bad boss can break trust. A bad boss can break productivity. A bad boss can break creativity and innovation. A bad boss can break confidence, morale, and any kind of joy we find at work.

Ultimately, a bad boss can break our spirits.

Let me be clear: this book isn't for the horrible, despised, worst of the worst of the bad bosses. It's not for the ones who have caused so much hurt and harm and wreaked absolute havoc on their organizations. It's not for the ones who have made headlines and contributed to destroying their companies' reputations as well as their own. It's not for the ones who know they are bad bosses and don't care. It's not for the ones who believe "bad bosses" are a necessary evil to growing a company's bottom line.

Those individuals will likely never read this book.

This book is for the rest of us. Because truth be told, we all have the capability, the potential, the possibility of becoming a bad boss. Whether we are just starting early in our career, or we are entering the C-suite, the environment we operate in, the circumstances we find ourselves in, and whom we work with every single day can tip the scales from "good boss" to "bad boss." And, what's happening in our homes can seep into our workplaces, as the line between home and work continues to get blurred. And in some cases, that line disappears all together.

I have worked in large public companies. I have worked in smaller, privately held companies. I have coached hundreds upon hundreds of leaders. I have been the confidant to many a CEO, founder, and board member. I have worked across functions, including product development and marketing and human resources, in global functions and in smaller, regional markets. I have worked across many different industries, including beauty, food and beverage, software as a service, and more. I have spent time in the public sector, private sector, and also with nonprofit organizations. And what I have discovered is this: bad bosses can exist anywhere. While some industries may have a reputation for creating exceptionally bad bosses, the truth is that they can be working and failing at leading anywhere, at any time.

I'll share 13 examples of bad bosses many of us have had to survive firsthand. Each chapter will open with a powerful bad boss story that I have experienced during my career in Corporate America. We'll go through a number of bad boss behaviors including micromanaging, ruling with fear, being completely disengaged, gossiping, stealing credit for work, creating constant fire drills, spreading toxic positivity, and much more.

Then we'll analyze each of these scenarios, asking ourselves what makes them so bad. We'll do self-reflective exercises to get to the root of why bad bosses may behave this way and review practical tips on how we can show up as good, and maybe even great, leaders for our teams and our organizations.

As you read these stories, I hope it helps you reflect on how you are developing your own leadership style and how you want to show up for your teams. I hope what you learn here also helps you watch for what's happening on your own teams, and how you can coach and develop the next generation of good leaders in our organizations. Ultimately, this book is a resource guide for aspiring people leaders, current people leaders, and anyone committed to building inclusive, healthy, and positive workplaces where we can all contribute and thrive.

I have changed the details, names, and places to protect the identities of these bad bosses. I genuinely hope that many of these bad bosses are no longer bad and that it was a temporary phase for them, like it was for me. My intent is not to shame, name, blame, or demonize any of them. My intent is to share these examples so the rest of us don't repeat the mistakes bad bosses make. And that we become good leaders, and even go on to be great ones.

Throughout this book, I will also share my lived experience as a woman of color. I have had dozens on dozens on dozens of bosses in my career, and, quite frankly, I have lost count (particularly in those years when my boss left the organization, and I got another new boss, and in some cases, another new boss after that, too). Here's the thing: anyone can be a bad boss. And I also acknowledge we can be quick to label an individual a bad boss given certain biases we may have about that individual and the community they belong to. I am sure people have also been quick to label me as a bad boss, even in moments when the label may not have been earned. As we go through stories and examples, I will focus on the behaviors of bad bosses, and help you challenge your biases.

Bosses have so much power over us. Over our teams. And in our workplaces. And we, as bosses, have so much power over others. And ultimately, whether we realize this or not, we can often single-handedly determine the experience those around us have.

Bosses can make or break inclusion. It's not the policies, procedures, or employee handbooks ultimately that dictate and define our workplace culture. Our culture becomes defined by what each and every one of us are doing when no one is looking over our shoulders. And this is particularly true for the boss who can have so much power in our organizations, hopefully yielding that power for good.

Bad bosses aren't born bad. Bad bosses are made. We become a product of our circumstances. Some of these bad boss behaviors don't just magically happen or appear. Some of these bad boss behaviors are in reaction to experiences from our childhood. Some of these bad boss behaviors are learned from bad bosses we once upon time reported to. And some of these bad boss behaviors are a reaction to the current environment we are operating in. We can become so desperate to survive our circumstances we slowly become that bad boss we had once vowed we would never be.

So, let's remember that the devil emails at midnight.

Let's make sure that devil doesn't become you.

1

The Boss Who Never Had Any Time for Me . . . Except at Midnight

I was so excited to meet my new boss.

Apparently, the feeling wasn't mutual.

I had landed a summer internship at one of the most coveted Fortune 500 employers. Hundreds of business school students from around the world were vying to have this big-name employer on their résumé. I knew being at this company would be a career game changer, so I was determined to get a spot in that intern class.

I missed my MBA classes at Duke University to participate in a week-long interview process at the company's campus, which mirrored a small town (including artificial ponds, a dry cleaner, an on-site childcare center, and more). I participated in marketing case study presentations, workshops on networking and crafting résumés, and career coffee chats with managers and division presidents. I was assigned to a team with four other students from other schools, whom I had never met. We were given a project to complete in less than 48 hours, culminating in a final presentation to a panel of leaders, who served as judges. We then had a final day of seven one-on-one interviews before we were transported back in large white vans to the airport.

I landed and marched back into my apartment in Durham, inhaled a stale bag of Cheetos, collapsed onto the bed, and slept for a solid 11 hours.

That following week, when I was back in classes, rushing from statistics to corporate strategy, I received a voicemail from a recruiter letting me know that I was in. I was officially a summer intern! I couldn't wait to get started and to meet my boss for the summer.

Our internship program kicked off on a sunny Monday in June. After a long day of onboarding sessions, we all piled into the cafeteria. We were greeted by bouncy balloons, lots of strangers smiling and waving, and a make-your-own sundae bar. I anxiously swirled around some rainbow sprinkles with the melted vanilla ice cream as I peered around for my new boss. I felt a tap on my shoulder.

"Hi, Mita. Welcome to campus. I'm Jeff, here to bring you up to the third floor."

"Hi," I said smiling. "Are you . . ."

"No," he laughed. "I'm not your boss for the summer. She didn't have time to come welcome you today, so you are stuck with me. Come on," he said, waving me on and instructing me to dump my melted sundae in the trash along the way. While everyone else's boss came to the intern welcome reception, my boss was apparently just too busy to come and greet me.

Back at his desk, he handed me an onboarding binder that included my summer internship project. "I'm sorry you got stuck with the Devil as your manager. At least it's only for this summer."

"The . . . Devil . . . ?" I asked confused.

"Her last name rhymes with the Devil, so that's why we call her that. She might be one of the worst bosses I have ever had."

I stared at the words *Welcome Mita* on my onboarding binder. My stomach sank. I wished I had finished that ice cream.

Jeff was one of three marketing managers on the Devil's team. Jeff resigned a week later. The second marketing manager, Tessa, left two weeks after Jeff. And then Tate, the third marketing manager, was rotated to another division the same week Tessa left. I was the only one left on the Devil's team. The summer intern.

Jeff's parting words to me were this: "She will never have time for you. She doesn't have time for anyone. The Devil will only make time for you at midnight. So, whatever you do, don't fall into the trap of emailing her back at night. Good luck."

Jeff's words came back to haunt me approximately 10 days later. With her entire team of marketing managers gone, the Devil started emailing me. At midnight. It was apparently the only time she had for me given her very busy schedule.

At first it was one or two or three emails. They would come in a flurry, one right after another, between the hours of 10 p.m. and 12 a.m. and sometimes later, when she appeared to be frantically clearing out her inbox. I tried to stay firm and not respond when the emails did pop up on my phone. The first few nights, I ignored them and went back to sleep. But my anxiety grew that I wouldn't get a full-time offer with the clock counting down my limited time as an intern. I started responding to her emails in the late evening hours.

With the Devil's entire team now gone, I was the only one left standing. I arrived at 7:30 a.m. sharp in the office, pulling into the campus parking lot and pretty much the same spot day after day. I would grab my Earl Gray tea from the cafeteria and head straight to my desk. During the hours of 8 a.m. to 5 p.m., I was the team's only marketing manager. I was doing all the full-time work of the three team members who had escaped her. Writing creative briefs, working with supply chain on cost savings initiatives, collaborating with other brands on promotions across category, signing off on product samples, working with finance on price increases and more. I zipped back and forth to and from meetings, raced to grab my lunch before the cafeteria closed or be stuck with a dreaded Kashi bar, crossed my legs tight and held my pee during meetings while feverishly taking notes, pecked away at the keyboard to send follow-up emails, and ran back to my desk to get samples. All the while, I waited to bump into her. To see her. To get a smile, a wave, a hello, a thank-you, anything to make me feel like she saw me, and I was appreciated.

I was like a golden retriever, pacing around the Devil's office, waiting for her to arrive in the mornings. I would eventually have to leave for a meeting, and then circle back to her office again in search of her. I would see her office door closed and her assistant would tell me to come back in 15 minutes. Only to return and find she was gone again. I would watch her race by my desk in a flurry and I would try to chase after her. I even tried to chase her out of the building one evening and she was just too quick for me, driving off in her car before I could say hello. I would wave at her in the cafeteria, try to follow her as she headed to a meeting, and try to go by her office to see if she was back in there. I was loyal and desperate for time with her in the office.

Most evenings, I would head to a summer intern event sponsored by the company, where I heard others talk about their incredible summers and their supportive managers. I would chug a cheap glass of Chardonnay and head back home. I would work on my summer internship project from 8 p.m. onwards. The final project presentation in front of the intern judging committee would determine if I would get an offer or not. As I worked late into the evening hours on my project, the pings would begin in my inbox. One by one emails from the Devil, sometimes a dozen or more at a time.

> *"Can you reach out to Ariel?"*
> *"This invoice needs to be paid."*
> *"Samples need to be sent out to buyers no later than Friday."*
> *"The share report is now due on Wednesdays. See attached for format changes."*
> *"See email chain below. Deck inputs due on Tuesday by noon."*

Sometimes it was a direct request. Sometimes there was an FYI. Sometimes there was no detail. Just emails forwarded along, and I had to play detective to figure out what to do.

There was never a *Hi, hello, how are you doing, are you enjoying your summer internship?* or *How can I be helping you?*

I worked at that company, working for the Devil, for 11 weeks for that summer internship.

In that time, I had two 15-minute meetings with my boss.

In the first meeting, she finally met with me five weeks into my internship. She didn't ask me how I was doing, or how the internship was going. She rattled off about 10 items she needed me to complete by the end of the week, with no direction or explanation. I scrambled to type as fast as I could all the requests. She then got a phone call and her assistant escorted me out of her office.

In the second meeting, which was the second to last week of my internship, she got up and left after seven minutes of me asking for feedback on my final internship presentation. She provided input on two slides. And then she said she had something more important to attend to. More important than helping to review my materials, which would decide whether or not I would get a full-time offer to join the company.

She then attended my final intern presentation and spent most of the time scrolling on her phone.

And finally, she had a 30 minute lunch with me at the company cafeteria during my last week and didn't offer to pay for my $5.25 turkey and Swiss cheese wrap. Other summer interns had their bosses take them out for lunch at a fancy Italian restaurant off campus.

At that lunch, she asked me to stay on full-time. "You don't even have to finish your MBA program," she laughed. "You can just join my team right now and dive into your marketing career."

I stared at her incredulously. I took a big bite of my wrap as she chattered on and on. This was the most time I ever spent with the Devil, and I witnessed the charm ooze right out of her. She was animated, telling me all the reasons to join her full-time right now and leave my MBA program.

"Thank you for the opportunity," I said wiping the mayonnaise off my mouth after she finally finished talking. "I'll be headed back next week to school."

Those 11 weeks of surviving the Devil paid off. I ended up getting a full-time offer to return to the company. My obsession with getting that company name on my résumé was closer to becoming a reality. And in a small silver lining, I received a text from Jeff several months later that said: "She's gone."

By the time I returned, the Devil was no longer working there.

★★★★★★★★

Years later, the question I continue to ponder is this: *Why didn't she have time for me?*

Time is the most precious commodity we have. It's the one thing we never seem to have enough of. We are bombarded with productivity hacks, systems, techniques, and advice from self-help gurus on how to squeeze more time out of our days. It's the

one thing we complain quietly or loudly about in our relationships: "You never have time for me." It's the one thing we know
is finite and yet we often stay in denial that for each and every
one of us, time will run out.

As individuals, we all want to be seen. In our workplaces,
most of us want to be seen by our bosses. We want them to
come by our desks and say hello. We want them to wave at us in
the hallway. We want them to drop us quick "hope you had a
good weekend" and "just checking in to see if you need anything" notes in Slack. We want them to spend time with us in
larger meetings, and in smaller, one-on-one settings. As leaders,
when we give our time, we strengthen our relationships with
those we work with. When we don't give our time, our team
members may begin to question their value and if they even
belong here. And if we don't have time for our teams, we should
question why we are leading a team in the first place.

Why don't we make the time at work to connect with those
who need our support?

In coaching dozens upon dozens of leaders over the years, I
have heard the following reasons and more for why they don't
spend time with their team members:

"I am just so busy. I don't have time."

"They will figure it out on their own."

"I have more important things to deal with."

*"I don't want to meet with them to discuss the same pro-
ject again."*

*"I'm so tired of them complaining about how I don't have time
for them."*

*"My manager never met with me. This generation needs too
much hand holding and coddling."*

*"Honestly, I find one of my managers incredibly annoying and
try to avoid them at all costs."*

"Didn't I just meet with them two weeks ago?"

My former boss is an extreme version of a bad boss who didn't understand the importance and value of giving and receiving time. By consistently emailing in the late evening hours, she also made it clear that she was available and willing to give snippets of time on her schedule and availability. And even when she did send me those emails, it was because she needed something from me. I finally came to accept our relationship was a one-way street. And as a result of her not giving her time, her team felt disgruntled, ignored, neglected, and unhappy. They all ended up leaving her team.

Do You Make Time for Those Who Work with You?

We might think we are making time for our teams. What would they say about how available we make ourselves? Consider the following as you review your schedule for the week, the next few weeks, or over the next quarter:

- How often do you meet with your entire team?
- How often do you have one-on-ones with direct reports?
- Do you do skip-level meetings to get to know other individuals on your broader team?
- Do you consistently prioritize meeting with your own boss, your peers, and other senior leaders over your team?
- When you cancel meetings with team members, do you offer an explanation?
- Do you connect with your team over Slack or email only when you need something?
- Do you give your time equally to everyone on your team?
- Are there some team members you meet with more frequently? Because you like them, have known them longer, or have a shared hobby or interest in common?

Making time for our teams, and offering our full attention, is one of the biggest ways we can show up as better leaders. Here's a framework I use when thinking about finding more time with my team.

Free Up Time

Start with freeing the time up on your calendar so you can spend meaningful moments with your team members. For newer leaders, balancing how they show up and give time to their teams while managing their own schedules can be a big challenge. They might be so focused on being "a leader" and spread themselves too thin, assuming their team can function without them. Even more experienced leaders can fall into the trap of focusing on themselves. They fail to recognize that their biggest job as a leader is to develop more leaders.

When I am at work, I want to make sure I am spending my time on the highest-value activities. Good leaders know that spending quality time with your teams can help improve employee morale and engagement, build stronger team bonds, overcome communication challenges, and create a more inclusive workplace.

So when it comes to my calendar, I ask myself this simple question: *Why am I in this meeting?*

I like to channel tidying expert Marie Kondo when thinking about how I declutter my calendar. We can start by proactively removing these meetings:

- Those where work can be done A-sync, work that should be automated, work that does not need to be reviewed or discussed live
- Reoccurring ones that were never revisited and are still on the calendar
- Those with no agenda or objective, or you have no idea why it's on your calendar

- Those where the decision-maker needs to be there and can't attend
- Those where an ambassador on your team can attend as a leadership opportunity

Remember the balance of FOMO (the fear of missing out) versus JOMO (the joy of missing out). Just because we are "the boss" doesn't mean we have to be in every single meeting. (In another chapter, we will tackle how to avoid the micromanaging tendencies of bad bosses, like the need to attend every single meeting.)

By proactively making space for high-value activities, you can take back control of your calendar and make time for your team. As the leader, you also then role model how you want to use your time and how you want your team to be using their own time at work as well.

Focus on How to Connect

Next, focus on how to connect and make the most of the time you have. Offering others your time can be about meeting face-to-face, and it can also be about leveraging technology we have at our disposal, so our teams feel seen and recognized.

There are many ways to be present for your team and give them more of your time:

- Meet with your team members one-on-one every week, or twice a month, depending on size of the team.
- Gather your broader team for quarterly or biannual off-sites, with clear objectives.
- Catch up over coffee, breakfast, or lunch in groups of three or four (remember not everyone drinks alcohol or feels comfortable drinking with their boss) where you can talk about anything but work (this can be done live or virtual.)
- Do skip-level meetings, where you give time to your direct reports' team members.

- Provide feedback on past presentations or projects, either in person or in writing.
- Coach through mistakes after a presentation or team discussion.
- Send an audio message or a Slack or brief email to provide an update.
- Prep a team member for a presentation, reviewing their talking points.
- Spontaneously check in via Slack or email; send quick personal notes as you get to know them. (For example, "Hope your daughter had a great basketball try-out." "Thanks again for the restaurant recommendation." "Look forward to hearing about your trip when you are back.") Remember to include some sort of small detail, because a *hi, how are you?* message might unintentionally trigger panic. Why is my boss reaching out? Do they need something?
- Embrace the lost art of a handwritten note: a simple sticky note on a desk or a handwritten note sent in the mail to showcase your gratitude for their contributions.

Remember, don't make this a check-the-box exercise. When you make the time to meet with them, stay focused and present. This means stay off devices, minimize distractions, and be present when you are making time for them. When you start to become present and available, others will follow your lead.

Are You Guilty of Emailing at Midnight?

If emailing early morning or late evening hours is the only time you have for your team, it's even more of a reason to re-evaluate how you spend your time at work. Consider the following:

(continued)

(continued)

- Do you consistently forward emails with no text or explanation because you are too busy regardless of what time it is?
- Do you wake up thinking about work at night or early morning hours, and you send that email so you won't forget?
- Do you consistently expect everyone on your team to operate around your schedule and when you have availability? Or only certain team members?

As a mother, I have often worked early or late hours in my career on global teams to catch up on work when I am dealing with a sick child, sports activities, caregiver out sick, dinner and bedtime, and more.

Here's what I think about:

- Have I conveyed to my team my schedule, particularly if I have team members working in different time zones? Have I let them know I don't expect them to respond to my emails, Slacks, or other forms of communication right away?
- Why do I need to send emails and updates to my team now? Have I considered what it might feel like to receive a barrage of emails from my boss in the late evening hours? Am I able to work offline and delay when I send or ask for things?
- Should I hold to send that email when I have slept more and have more time to think about what I want to say?
- If I delay sending these emails until the morning, how will my team feel when they open their inboxes and see

a dozen emails from me? Do I need to send all these emails or can I communicate some of this information live? Can sharing these updates or requests wait?

Remember, as the leader of the team, you set the tone for when and why we communicate.

Fend Off and Stay Firm

Fend off meetings from reappearing on your calendar once you have decided they are not a high-value activity. Fending off and staying firm also means doing the following:

- Stick to your framework to keep your time free and protect it. This means not just accepting every meeting that comes your way. This also means revisiting on a bimonthly basis what new meetings are being added and why. Like when managing my wardrobe and buying things I don't really need, I ask myself, "If a new meeting is being added, what meeting is being removed?"
- Protect the time you have dedicated to team members; let anyone overseeing your calendar know the importance of this time.
- Avoid cancellation of time dedicated to your team; when it happens cancel with explanation and reschedule (don't keep rescheduling and rescheduling, pushing this unintentionally months out.)

Following this simple framework can help you show up as a better leader. Because imagine coming to work every day and wondering if your boss even knows you are there. They never have time for you. If we can't make time for our teams, we likely shouldn't be leading. Making time for our teams is one of the most important ways we can build inclusive team environments and ultimately more inclusive workplaces.

Tips on Making Time for Your Team

- Reflect on what holds you back from making time for your team.
- Audit and review how much time you currently do make for your team. Then ask your team how they would like to see you make yourself more available.
- Use and adapt the framework:
  - Free up time:
    - Start by freeing the time up on your calendar so you can spend meaningful moments with your team.
  - Focus on how to connect:
    - Make the most of the time you have.
  - Fend off and stay firm:
    - Fend off meetings from reappearing on your calendar once you have decided they are not a high-value activity.
- Send handwritten notes as another way to connect versus relying only on technology.
- Communicate changes in your schedule and why you may be reaching out at late hours, especially when working on a global team.
- Ask yourself if you really need to send that email, that text, or that Slack at midnight or if it can wait.

2

The Boss Who Didn't Want to Call Me by My Name . . . So He Renamed Me Mohammed

When I first started out in my career, I never anticipated that the bullies from the playgrounds and classrooms would follow me into Corporate America. That they would be there, patiently waiting for me. In the cubicles, on Zoom, in the conference rooms. Casually hanging out by the coffee bar, first to show up at the happy hour, and always lurking around, ready to pounce in the hallways.

And that the bully, who would push you off the tire swing at the neighborhood park to claim their spot, wearing a big smile, could end up one day being your boss.

After I parted ways with the Devil that summer, a few years later, I encountered the first of several bad bully bosses I would end up working for. The memory of that very first bad bully boss lingers and lingers and lingers. Even after you have experienced and survived more bad bully bosses, you never forget the very first time you are bullied in Corporate America.

Enter the Sheriff.

With many of these bad bosses, I wasn't the first to uncover their reputation for being bad. In a number of cases, someone before me had survived them and nicknamed them before I had a chance to. So, I can't take any credit for the naming of the Sheriff.

I had never met anyone quite as tall as the Sheriff. His height helped him keep tabs of the comings and goings of everything that happened in the office, beyond just our division. He was so tall he could easily look over high cubicle walls as he strolled on by, eavesdropping on conversations. He could peer into the very top of the unfrosted windows of a conference room to see if confidential meetings were taking place. He could quickly scan a happy hour crowd, a packed conference, or the quarterly town hall audience to see who was and wasn't there. Some days you could just see him walking around hour after hour, circulating on different floors, monitoring, investigating, and gathering information of what was happening. He also had a network of deputies who would report back to him on any critical information he missed, particularly if he was traveling or had been trapped in a conference room in an all-day meeting calibrating talent.

The other striking characteristic of the Sheriff was that he had hair so blond it almost looked white, accompanied with pale skin and intense blue eyes. He looked like a direct descendant from House Targaryen of King's Landing, from *The Game of Thrones*. Unlike the reputation of Aegon Targaryen, the first king of the fictional land of Westeros, who was known to be quiet and withdrawn, the Sheriff was incredibly friendly and social. He was the bully everyone liked.

The Sheriff was charismatic. He was socially intelligent; he could read people well as he enrolled deputies into his network. He loved chatting and getting to know people. He cleverly remembered small details they had shared about their new French bulldog, their daughter's basketball travel team tryouts, their favorite happy hour drink—gin and tonic with extra lime—their family reunion coming up in Naples, Florida, and more. He liked connecting with people and they liked him. He had the ability to make his leaders, his direct reports, and his colleagues feel seen.

Early on, the Sheriff had studied me like a textbook and recognized that I would be an easy bullying target on his team. I was more of a quiet leader, struggling with overcoming my shyness at work. I was busy with tapping away at the keyboard in my cubicle, determined to prove myself on this new team. It's like the Sheriff knew what my father had once told me, "Keep your head down, work hard, and stay out of trouble." I had too much work to do and no time to make work friends and become part of his deputy network. I was also one of a handful of women of color in a division of approximately 100 people. So, at this point in my career, I certainly wasn't going to cause any trouble for myself or others and jeopardize my job.

The Sheriff once wrote in my performance review: *I can tell the lights are on but not sure anyone's home. Her inability to participate in meetings will make it next to impossible for her to become a director here.* The Sheriff could serve up the most devastating feedback with a smile on his face. Like the bully who pushed you off the tire swing with a big grin. When I asked him about the feedback in person, he said with a Joker-esque smile, "Don't worry;

everything is fine. You worry too much. There's no rush to get promoted, after all."

The Sheriff once told me I could work from home on Fridays only if I took on another massive project that he knew I didn't have the capacity to do well. (Maybe I could do the project well, if I worked both Saturdays and Sundays.) He wanted me to be the head of the summer intern committee. This move would also make him look good with absolutely no effort required on his end. Having once been an intern myself, I couldn't begin to imagine all of the logistics and details and planning that had to go into the committee. Not to mention trying to get other colleagues to volunteer and lead different subcommittees. It would be like trying to get a dozen or more toddlers to walk in the same direction with a walking rope while half of them were in the middle of meltdowns.

At that time, my commute to the office was approximately two hours (or more on some days, I had to take the subway, the train, and then a shuttle) each way. I had a friend who worked in another division, lived in the same city as me with the same commute, and she and other colleagues were able to work from home every single Friday. Leading this summer intern committee was additional office work that I knew I couldn't take on. I still needed to learn the basics of my marketing job: forecasting, budgeting, writing campaign briefs, and more. And if I took this on, my day job would suffer.

But the Sheriff wouldn't budge.

"Just say yes to the summer intern committee and you can work from home on Fridays, no problem," he said, flashing another smile. So, I decided to continue to come into the office every single Friday.

Then the Sheriff, after several weeks of working for him, decided to target what he had assessed was my Achilles heel: my name.

When I graduated from business school, and started in Corporate America, I decided to reclaim my full name. Madhumita (pronounced ma-dhoo-me-tha) Mallick. For most of my life, I had just gone by Mita. My cultural upbringing taught me to put others' comfort ahead of my own. I stopped bothering to teach people how to say my full name or demand they learn; I just chopped it.

"Honestly, keep going by Mita Mallick," the career counselor coached me, striking through my name in red on my résumé. "No one can pronounce this; you won't get callbacks." I understood what she shared: I was used to having my name be mispronounced, misspelled, and even repeatedly be mistaken for the only other Brown woman in my town or team. My name had been a source of anxiety, embarrassment, and shame. And I wanted to reclaim it as a source of pride, my identity and heritage, and joy. Many of us seem to forget that our names were given to us by someone who had big hopes and dreams for us. I wanted to embrace and honor my full name.

When it came to my name, the Sheriff decided not to repeatedly and intentionally mispronounce my name. He decided not to give me a nickname that was short for something else. He decided to completely rename me. Because he couldn't pronounce my full name Madhumita, and didn't want to learn how to pronounce it. He decided to rename me and call me Mohammed. Because he could and he wanted to.

"Mohammed, did you pull that Nielsen data the team asked for?"

"Mohammed, can you join us for the 4 p.m. call?"

"Mohammed, make sure the agency knows to dial in for the kickoff."

He called me Mohammed in our one-on-one meetings behind closed doors. He shouted Mohammed down the hall to get my attention. He called me this name in front of my peers, his peers, and even his own boss. The bullying, like the flu, became contagious. Two of his deputies also started calling me Mohammed, waving as they passed by my cubicle.

Some days, I went to the bathroom stall to quietly cry.

Some days, I would take alternative, longer exits out of the building to avoid walking by his office.

Some days, I called in sick. Even then, he once typed an email to me addressed as Mohammed. I couldn't escape it.

"You can call me Mita," I once mustered up the courage in his office after weeks of this happening. "That would be fine."

"Oh, Mohammed is funny. Everyone loves it. Don't be so sensitive!" He said flashing his famous smile.

I'm embarrassed to admit that for many, many, many weeks I responded to a name that was not my own. I stayed because I wanted that big company brand on my résumé. I stayed because everyone else around me seemed to be doing so well in their jobs. I stayed because I thought I was making a bigger deal of it that I should have.

And I slowly felt myself disappearing. I found it exhausting to do the bare minimum at work. I wasn't interested in speaking up and proposing new ideas. With the support of a friend, I finally mustered the strength to update my résumé. I quit and moved on to another company. The day I resigned he acted shocked and hurt, like I had done something wrong. The Sheriff had me escorted out of the building, watching me gather my things and exit, claiming I was working for a direct competitor (which wasn't true).

I never saw him or spoke to him again.

Until.

Years later, I was at the annual Ad Council dinner, a large industry event, where the tables were packed. And as I sat down, right behind me, at another table was the Sheriff. I froze. I felt like I was going to vomit all over the breadbasket. I couldn't feel my legs. I felt a massive headache take over. I was panicked he might see me and try to talk to me. I grabbed my bag, jumped in an Uber and escaped, texting a friend the whole time.

When my first book *Reimagine Inclusion: Debunking 13 Myths to Transform Your Workplace* made the *Wall Street Journal* and *USA Today* best-seller lists, I had many people reach out with notes of congrats. One of the Sheriff's former bosses, whom I hadn't spoken to since I quit that company years ago, reached out to say congrats and "how proud" they were of me. They asked if there was anything they could do to support me.

The only thing I wanted to ask was this: "Did you ever tell him to stop calling me Mohammed? Did you ever tell him to just call me by my name?"

★★★★★★★

The act of being "renamed Mohammed" at work is not as uncommon as you may think.

According to the 2023 Workplace Harassment & Misconduct Insights study, 51% of employees have witnessed or experienced workplace bullying.[1] And who are these bullies then? Almost two-thirds—65%—of the bullies are in fact the toxic boss.[2] Microaggressions, like the one I experienced repeatedly, can become a manifestation of bullying. They deplete our energy, chip away at our confidence, and make us question our contributions at work. Microaggressions can affect our careers in multiple ways, including increased burnout and decreased job satisfaction. It can take significant emotional, physical, and sometimes financial resources to recover from the impact of repeated harm in the workplace.

Most of us are hired for our expertise and our track record of success. We want to come to work and be at 100% capacity; we want to make meaningful contributions. But imagine if your boss is the one teasing you about your accent, consistently mistaking you for the only other Black colleague on the team, questioning if you know how to use technology because you are an "experienced" hire, telling you to smile more often during your performance review, and more. Given these factors in the environment, your 100% capacity to contribute can drop to 75% to even 50%. Rather than being able to focus on the work you were hired to do, your energy is instead spent worrying about what your boss might do or say next. And wondering whether or not you actually belong at your organization.

If this happens to multiple individuals over time, the cumulative effect can be a huge drop in productivity for an organization. Individuals feel less connected to others and less connected to the work. Imagine the hours lost and wasted that can't be recovered. Seven out of 10 employees say they would be upset by a microaggression, and 50% of employees would consider resigning.[3] When talent walks out the door, the cost is higher than we might think. According to Gallup, the cost of replacing an individual employee who resigns can be anywhere from one-half to two times their annual salary—and that's a conservative estimate.[4] In totality, US businesses lose close to $1 trillion every year to employees quitting.

Toxic bosses can negatively affect the bottom line. Inclusive leaders can stop productivity-killing microaggressions in their tracks.

Many of us reflecting on the story of the Sheriff are thinking that we would never say or do anything like that. That he is an extreme version, a caricature, of a bad boss. That individuals like him don't work in our organizations. But far too often they do work among us. Because their bosses dismiss their behavior.

Consider the following statements you may have overheard or said to a colleague:

No, I mean where are you actually from?

Is that your real hair? You sure do like to change your hairstyle a lot.

You look so young. Are you sure you are not an intern?

Oh, well, you look so normal. We all have some kind of disability, don't we?

Do we really have to make such a big deal about Pride month? We have so many deadlines to meet.

How did you learn to speak English so well?

The promotion can wait. Don't you want to think about starting a family now?

Now self-reflect on the following questions:

- Do we actively keep a lookout for microaggressions on our teams?
- Do we believe colleagues when they share their experiences?
- Do we consider microaggressions to be hurtful, negatively affecting productivity?
- Do we think that individuals are being hypersensitive, blowing things out of proportion, and making a big deal out of an innocent comment or casual remark?
- Do we dismiss concerns about a boss who is the root cause of microaggressions because they are a "high performer"? Are their feelings and their comfort more important than those they have harmed?

The Devil never made time for me. The Sheriff unfortunately made time for me in a different way. He knew I was new to the team and already isolated. He strategically made the calculation to make me his target. He was incredibly politically skilled. He could do bad things really well and somehow get away it, even with his peers and bosses watching. I never reported him to human resources because I didn't see the point. Somewhere along the way I had also internalized that children's nursery rhyme: *Sticks and stones may break my bones, but names can never hurt me.* I failed to realize until it was too late that names, and microaggressions, can crush your spirit.

Why Do We Use the Term *Microaggressions?*

In the 1970s, Dr. Chester M. Pierce introduced the term *racial microaggressions.*[5] Dr. Derald Wing Sue, who expanded on Pierce's research, defines a *racial microaggression* as one of the "everyday insults, indignities and demeaning messages sent to people of color by well-intentioned white people who are unaware of the hidden messages being sent to them."[6] Psychologists, including Sue, have worked to amplify the concept to include subtle or indirect expressions of racism, sexism, ageism, ableism, and more, and how this affects various communities.

While I use the word *microaggressions* in this book, which has been widely adopted by many, I still struggle with the term. The *micro* part may reinforce to some leaders that these acts are harmless, small, trivial, and insignificant. What's the opposite of a microaggression? A macroaggression? And who gets to decide the impact and severity of the hurt and harm we endure? Because the macro effect of microaggressions in our workplaces is clear.

Ibram X. Kendi wrote in *How to Be an Antiracist* that he no longer uses the term *microaggression.* "I detest its component parts—'micro' and 'aggression,'" he wrote. "A persistent daily low hum of racist abuse is not minor."[7] Ruchika T. Malhotra wrote in her *Harvard Business Review* piece, "We Need to Retire the Term 'Microaggressions,'" that she prefers the term *exclusionary behaviors.*[8] Regardless of what we call them, microaggressions are real. Toxic bosses deny their impact while often perpetuating them in

---

our workplaces. Good leaders stop microaggressions in their tracks and build an inclusive culture where we can all contribute and thrive.

As a leader, here's a framework I use on my journey to stop microaggressions on my teams.

Be Open to Learning

It takes humility to admit we don't understand a phrase, a term, or a comment someone else has made. And we can't interrupt and stop microaggressions if we can't recognize it happening and the message it may be sending. Our job is to continue to upskill ourselves on behaviors and language we aren't familiar with. Focus on the following:

- Research and Google terms we aren't familiar with. Sometimes we might hear something that makes us uncomfortable, and we aren't sure why. Take the time to learn. Follow up by asking those we have trusted relationships with clarifying questions once we have done our research.
- Self-reflect and consider if a comment, joke, or question is funny or is not funny. Observe who is laughing and who is feeling uncomfortable and seems to be withdrawing from the conversation or meeting.
- Watch for comments or remarks that are targeting, singling out, or dismissing one person or a group of individuals. Does this individual belong to a historically marginalized community? Do others on the team perceive this individual to be "different"?
- Listen and believe what individuals have to share about their experiences when it comes to microaggressions.
- Share what we learn with others and role model education for our teams.

Determine When to Intervene

It's important to consider the context, the power dynamics involved, and the specific situation when determining when to intervene. Here's what I consider:

Intervening in the moment when:
- I understand the microaggression that has taken place.
- I want to set the tone in front of others. "Let's take a moment to go around the room and introduce ourselves again before we continue this meeting. So, we can make sure we are all pronouncing everyone's name correctly."
- I realize I have done something wrong. "I'm sorry I used the wrong pronouns when referring to Caleb earlier. I'm sorry, Caleb. That won't happen again."

Intervening afterwards when:
- I don't fully understand or am not even aware that a microaggression has taken place. I need to take time to educate myself and then intervene.
- I want to have a one-on-one conversation with the person who was affected to check in on them first.
- I want to be engaged in one-on-one dialogue with the person who caused harm to have an honest conversation. This may be a moment to educate them. Or, if they are repeatedly targeting someone on the team, a more serious conversation needs to be had potentially with the help of human resources with clear consequences.

Hold Individuals Accountable

"The culture of any organization is shaped by the worst behavior the leader is willing to tolerate," says Steve Gruenert and Todd Whitaker, authors of *School Culture Rewired*.[9] We have to ask ourselves, what behaviors are we willing to overlook and tolerate at the expense of eroding our culture?

We must hold individuals accountable for their behavior. Hold yourself accountable for what you say and do as well and set the tone for the team. A lack of accountability erodes not only team culture but also over time erodes your leadership brand, negatively affecting your long-term career prospects.

We should also encourage space for apologies and education so we can learn and grow together. And make it clear that any instance of repeat behavior won't be tolerated. Some toxic bosses just need to move on. They may not need another executive coach; they may just need therapy.

The reality is many of us reading this book will never become a boss like the Sheriff. And we have the power and responsibility as leaders to make sure that a bad boss like the Sheriff has absolutely no place on our teams or in our organizations.

The 5Ds of Bystander Intervention

Over the years, I have had the privilege to work with Right to Be, a nonprofit that started with a simple idea: a blog to collect stories of street harassment. They created an international movement, teaching bystander intervention trainings to stop harassment across the world. I highly recommend educating yourself with their free resources and bringing them as a paid partner into your organization. Microaggressions can be part of a pattern of bullying. Bullying can then turn into harassment when it is aimed at someone because of their "race, color, religion, sex (including sexual orientation, gender identity, or pregnancy), national origin, age, disability, or genetic information (including family medical history) and is illegal when proven as such." It's important as leaders to understand these differences and also recognize our role at times as bystanders in and out of the workplace.

Right to Be's framework focuses on the 5Ds model:

Distract: a subtle and creative way to intervene and interrupt the harassment

Delegate: asking a third party to help with intervening in harassment

Document: involves recording or taking notes on an instance of harassment

Delay: checking in on the target after the incident

Direct: responding directly, naming inappropriate behavior, confronting the person doing harm

For more details on this framework, please refer to Right to Be's resources: https://righttobe.org/our-training/.

Remember, we all have the right to be respected and valued in our workplaces.

Tips on Stopping Microaggressions on Our Teams

- Be open to learning about microaggressions and educate yourself on actions and behaviors you may not be familiar with.

- Understand that microaggressions can be part of a pattern of bullying, and bullying can then turn into harassment.

- Ask follow-up questions with those you have trusted relationships with, only after you have done the research.

- Share with your team members what you are learning.

- Watch for behaviors on your team and individual team members.

- Intervene during or after a microaggression takes place, remembering the context, power dynamics, and situation matters as you assess what to do.

- Hold yourself accountable on what you do, what you say, and what you role model.

- Encourage space for apologies and education so we can learn and grow together. Make it clear that any time of repeat behavior won't be tolerated, and ask human resources for support and help.

  - For more support on how to apologize in our workplaces, please refer to my first book, *Reimagine Inclusion: Debunking 13 Myths to Transform Your Workplace*.

3

The Boss Who Fell Asleep in Almost Every Meeting

When I was working for the Sheriff and frantically trying to plot my escape, a friend sounded the following alarm, evoking a famous quote: "Just don't jump from the frying pan into the fire. Choose your next assignment carefully." I remember smiling politely, as we sipped our Earl Grey teas, and then tucking that advice far, far away. It really wasn't relevant to my situation. Because could there even be a boss worse than the Sheriff?

Enter the Napper.

I received a call from a recruiter to interview with one of the biggest beauty brands in the world. I was freaking out, pacing around and around in circles in a small one-bedroom Manhattan apartment. This was my chance not only to break free from the Sheriff but also to catapult my career into a company that didn't often have job openings at my level, but didn't have the best Glassdoor reviews.

And I didn't have time to ask too many questions. The recruiter had called back, and I was set to go in to interview in exactly 48 hours. I raced to the Ann Taylor on Fifth Avenue, and had an associate there convince me to buy a very cool and pricey suit: a wrap black jacket with a pinkish beige chiffon skirt. I was ready to land this role. This job was mine.

I called in sick to the Sheriff and went in to interview with close to a dozen people, including my future boss. It was a long day, back-to-back, one meeting after another. There were a number of people I really enjoyed meeting with. They were curious about my background; they wanted to know what I thought about the latest competitive beauty products in the market; they gave me samples to take home with me. With each conversation, I was getting more and more excited. And then, toward the end of the day, I finally met with the person who would become my boss.

He was 15 minutes late.

He came with a Dunkin' Donuts coffee he slurped loudly for most of our 15 minutes together.

He went back and forth between seeming disinterested while scrolling on his phone and talking over me when I attempted to answer his questions.

He asked me what my favorite band was, if I drank coffee or tea, and if I had any food allergies.

He even told me he wasn't really into "beauty stuff" and this job paid his bills.

The interview could be summed up as underwhelming, uncomfortable, and at times a bit unbelievable (why did he need to know if I had food allergies if I was going to be supporting the eyeshadow, eyeliner, and mascara portfolio?).

The very next morning, I was back at work. Later that day, I snuck into the stairwell and answered a call from the recruiter. He made me an offer. He shared with me that his colleagues really enjoyed meeting with me. I said yes on the spot. I liked everyone—except for my future boss. And for some reason, after having survived the Sheriff, I wasn't too worried about that.

On my first day at my new job, I was there exactly at 7:59 a.m. in the lobby of a very nondescript tall Manhattan building. People pushed each other aside to hurry through the turn stalls, getting in line for the elevators. I waited at security for Maria, the vice president's assistant, who came to greet me with a big smile.

I settled into my cubicle that morning with my laptop, scrummaging through a big bag of product goodies. Some of the marketing managers took me to breakfast. They then brought me to the weekly staff meeting where I introduced myself. I followed someone to their product innovation kickoff meeting, then went to a cost-savings initiative task force. I was back at my cubicle, logging onto my laptop, filling out forms to make sure I would get paid on time and get health insurance. My boss was nowhere to be found.

He finally showed up at 10:30 a.m.

"Oh, you are here, hi," he said, surprised. He was rushing by my cubicle, then abruptly stopped. "I completely forgot it was your first day. I'm right here if you need anything," he said, motioning to the cubicle right next to him. I smiled, nodded, and said I was happy to be there.

An hour later, I stood up and walked several steps and knocked on his cubicle, peering in, "Hi, I was wondering how to . . ."

He was fast asleep in his chair. I was absolutely startled and scurried back to my seat. My brain couldn't process what I was seeing. It was the first time I had ever seen anyone asleep at work. It wouldn't be the last.

The Napper usually showed up between 10:30 a.m. and 11 a.m. Some days he would try to covertly sneak in, other days, he would walk in like he was a celebrity making an entrance in a music video. He would log in, call his wife to talk about dinner plans, check in with friends about fantasy football, and send me emails asking me for status updates even though we were within three feet of each other. He would gossip loudly, enlisting others to talk about how much "it sucked to work here." He would be gone by 4:00 p.m. at the latest, if not earlier, to catch his train. At least once a week he would leave for lunch around 1 p.m. with other colleagues he convinced to join him and just not come back to work. Our cubicles had high walls, so I couldn't actually see him. But I could hear him, chatting away and laughing on calls, occasionally typing, complete silence, and then on and off snoring.

The first time I saw him fall asleep in our staff meeting I stared at the cracks between the panels on the wooden floor. I looked up to lock eyes with another colleague who gestured in the Napper's direction and rolled his eyes. I soon came to realize that the Napper's behavior was the worst kept secret on the team.

The size of the meetings didn't matter to him; he dozed off in very large and small meetings. I presented our annual brand plan, watching him nap during my presentation. I watched him doze off dozens of times during our quarterly town hall meetings. He once had closed his eyes for several minutes in our VP's monthly meeting; she angrily shouted his name and asked him a question. He was startled, but not embarrassed, and gave a mumbled a response that had nothing to do with the question she had asked. He went back to looking at his phone shortly after.

I had no idea what the Napper worked on all day. I ran point on pretty much every single project. Some days he came to meetings, other days he didn't. Some weeks we had one-on-one check-ins where I would just rattle off what I was currently working on and he would just sit there. Some weeks he would cancel. He gave me a written mid-year review that said I was "meeting expectations," and that included lots of overwhelmingly positive feedback from my peers and cross-functional partners. I tried to schedule a live discussion about it, which he kept rescheduling over and over and over again until I finally let it fall off our calendars.

He went from being completely and comfortably disengaged to occasionally being highly agitated.

"Why wasn't I included in the kickoff for our second half innovation?" He accused me one day, standing in my cubicle.

I pulled up the calendar invite on my screen and pointed to his name. He had neither accepted nor declined my invitation for that meeting.

"Oh. Okay." He retreated back to his cubicle.

His lack of interest in work and in being a manager slowly chipped away at me. The only silver lining was his lack of interest in working gave me the opportunity to step up and fill the leadership void.

Maria, the team's assistant who also supported the vice president, sat in the cubicle directly across from the Napper. She wrinkled her nose in disgust whenever he walked by. "I have no idea how he still is employed here." Maria's sentiment was shared by many other colleagues. We all wondered how he could get away with it day after day, week after week, month after month. He had been working there for three years by the time I joined his team.

At first, I had empathy for the situation. I wondered: Did he have narcolepsy? Was he stuck sleeping on an uncomfortable couch every night because maybe he was fighting with his wife? Did he have a newborn we didn't know about? Was he struggling with a substance abuse problem? Was a family member ill? My mind often swirled with various scenarios of what could be causing the Napper's behavior at work.

Or was it just sheer boredom? Had he completely spiraled and was so disengaged that he just didn't care about his job anymore?

"He wasn't always like that," my colleague Sarah shared one day. "He used to really care about his job."

"Really?" I was in shock. "What do you mean?"

"They say he used to be a top performer. It apparently all changed when the new VP came, and he got turned down for that promotion. That's when the dozing off started."

Even after Sarah shared those details, I still wondered if there was something more to the Napper's backstory. And the what-if scenarios swirling in my head about what was happening officially ended that day I heard him on a call with a recruiter. I couldn't believe what I was hearing. I held my breath and got as close as I could to our shared cubicle wall. I sat there listening as some heels clicked-clacked by.

$150,000!!!

That's how much my boss, the Napper, made. I was doing his job, *and* my job, for a little more than half that amount.

He had spiraled so deep that he was taking calls from recruiters at work, not in a conference room, stairwell, or even on the sidewalk outside the building. He was openly interviewing for other external roles right from his desk.

And yet, after all that, the VP never fired him. She still let him stay.

After a year of surviving the Napper, a new vice president arrived to run our division. A few months later, on a late Tuesday afternoon, the new vice president called me into his office to let me know I had been promoted. I couldn't believe that my hard work had paid off. I was stunned and elated; I could now report directly into the new vice president. And someone who would go on to be one of the best leaders I ever worked for.

That evening, I toasted with colleagues with a glass of Prosecco at our favorite bar down the street from our offices. The Napper was nowhere to be seen; I was sure he had left the office hours before. Days later, the Napper sent me a short email that said, "Congrats and good luck." He never said anything in person. More promotions and restructuring happened in the division in the weeks to follow and my desk was moved to the other side of the floor. I was no longer sitting next to him.

I stopped tracking the comings and goings of the Napper. Until one day, about nine months later, we received an email from the vice president saying the Napper was moving on from the organization: *We wish him best of luck in his future endeavors.*

★★★★★

Years later, I still wonder the following: Why was my former boss allowed to repeatedly nap at work without any consequences?

According to Gallup's State of the Global Workplace report, "Employees who are not engaged or who are actively disengaged cost the world $8.8 trillion in lost productivity."[1] That's equal to 9% of global GDP. With so many employees disengaged, many of these individuals are also likely to be leading teams. Some of them could be actively disengaged and loudly quitting over and over again, every single day. They could be that bad boss. They could be in fact the Napper.

This isn't just about the occasional nap, refresh, or reset needed during the day. This isn't about the unrealistic expectation that individuals need to be fully engaged for every minute of every workday. This is about actively disengaged individuals who are vocal about disliking their jobs both in and outside of work. They often don't show up to work, and when they do, they don't attend meetings and aren't really present. They can be low energy, be bored, and be completely disinterested in the work and coaching their teams. Imagine the ripple effect actively disengaged bad bosses like the Napper can have on their teams.

Disengagement can spread. It can become contagious. Like a virus, it can rapidly spread to decrease engagement, erode trust on the team, and negatively affect productivity.

So as leaders, when we work with actively disengaged team members, why don't we intervene? Why don't we stop the downward spiral? And why do we let that person who just doesn't seem to care about work anymore stay longer than they should?

Here are some of the reasons:

- We don't want to go to the trouble of firing anyone. We'll wait for someone else to do it.
- We are waiting for the next round of layoffs; we'll put them on the list then.
- We believe this is just a phase and they will turn their attitude around.
- We are waiting for them to leave on their own.
- We have too many other business–critical issues to deal with.
- We don't think their behavior is as bad as Jennifer, who was a real pot stirrer.
- We are worried about our own job security.
- We see that their team's performing; this person's behavior must not be that big of a deal.

The question is, how long are we willing to put up with this behavior? And at what cost?

Human Resources Policies Alone Can't Solve for Disengaged Leaders

According to Kincentric (a Spencer Stuart company), human resources (HR) policies designed to create positive experiences and increase employee engagement and motivation fall flat when up against disengaged leaders.[2] Their research showed that "disengaged leaders actually neutralize the effectiveness" of these policies:

- Even when employees are formally acknowledged and included in an employee recognition program, "those working for disengaged leaders show no subsequent bump in engagement."
- Even after a promotion, "employees on teams led by disengaged leaders show no increase in engagement."
- Even when receiving a full bonus, employees working for disengaged leaders show no increase in engagement. By contrast, "employees working for engaged leaders show an increase in engagement even when getting a somewhat disappointing bonus."

Recognizing your employees, hard work and paying them more doesn't always cut it. Don't place the burden on HR to "fix disengagement." If you really want your employees to be motivated at work, start dealing with the disengaged leader, that bad boss they have to work for.

As leaders, it's our job to see if we can reengage those who are now disengaged at work. Here's a framework I have used during my career and as I have led teams and coached others.

Be a Mirror

Some may think the easy thing to do is to put an individual on a performance improvement plan and force them out of the company. Some may also just let the behavior slide, let it go, until they come to their senses or decide to leave on their own. This is an opportunity for you to be a mirror when it comes to their behavior:

- Make it a priority to take them out to lunch or coffee. Or find time that is not your usual one-on-one check-in meetings to talk to them.
- Be a mirror and remind them of their behavior. Focus on the facts, and not your feelings. Imagine if you had been recording them; what would you share back on what you had seen? Here's some language to consider:
  - I wanted to check in and see how you are doing and share some of the things that I have been observing lately.
  - Recently, I have noticed that you come in later in the morning and leave by mid-afternoon. I have noticed that you haven't attended our weekly staff meeting the last several weeks, and that you are mostly at your desk not interacting much with your team. I also had to send a number of follow-up reminders for the urgent deliverables our vice president needed.
  - I wanted to get your perspective on how you are feeling about work and if there's anything you feel comfortable sharing.

Allow Space for Them to Reveal What's Going On

When we allow space for individuals to reveal what's going on, we need to be prepared to hear the following:

- Feedback on our leadership styles, challenges with resourcing and budgets being cut, lack of clarity on career progression, believing they aren't being fairly compensated, dealing with low performers on their own team, and more

- Personal struggles, including dealing with divorce, loss of a loved one, a break-up, substance abuse and addiction, health issues, and more
- Lack of interest in the actual work and no longer believing in the vision of the organization

We may or may not agree with what is shared. When you allow them to share, you don't have to respond to everything. You can ask open-ended follow-up questions or simply thank them for sharing, letting them know you are processing the information.

Also, be prepared to be met with silence, no response, and a reluctance to share anything. If that's the case, you can say, "I am here to help. If there's something you would like to share now, or in a few days with me, please let me know." If they aren't willing to share and don't want your support, your next step should be to meet with HR. If they are actively disengaged, and unwilling to change, it's time for them to move on from the organization.

Ask Them What Has to Change

Professor Michael Murphy of Harvard University offers this powerful question for us to ask: "What could change at work for you to be excited again about working here?"[3]

You likely won't be able to change what they have revealed about the past, which may have led to their disengagement. What you can do is offer to help moving forward, and to listen to any feedback they share. Some of the feedback you may be able to action, and some of it not. And by asking this question, you are getting the individual to self-reflect on how they can take ownership for becoming more engaged at work.

Spark Their Interest in Learning Again

Being excited about being at work again can be tied to becoming more curious and learning. Help spark their interest in how they can continue to upskill themselves. If your organization has a budget to help support them in taking a course, take advantage of that. And if not, there's a wealth of free information available online. Help them narrow down what they want to learn more about, offer for them to shadow someone at work if possible, and ask if they can share back with the team what they are learning.

Create a Plan and Stick to It

If they are willing to work on their engagement, you need to create a plan and stick to it. Consider the following:

- How will you measure engagement? What specific leadership behaviors are you looking for them to work on? Will you check in with their team to see how their boss is doing?
- Are there clear work deliverables they need to meet moving forward?
- What's the timeline for the overall plan? Will you check monthly to track progress and what's the end date for the plan?

Some disengaged individuals may decide they want to recommit to the organization. Other disengaged individuals may come to their own conclusion that it's time for them to move on.

If this happens, work with HR to come back to them with a severance option and timeline for departure. Others may not want to leave on their own, and it's your job as a leader to help them with that transition. Leaving the organization may be ultimately what's in the best interest of their team and their own careers.

What Are the Signs You Are Disengaging at Work?

"When people are sleeping on the job, they are sending a signal," says Mark Royal, a Korn Ferry senior client partner specializing in employee engagement. "It's up to leaders to figure out what sort of signal."[4]

Most of us don't want to get to the point where we are actively disengaged and sleeping on the job. And employee engagement isn't binary; we don't just suddenly go from being actively engaged to actively disengaged. What are some early signs that we are becoming less connected to our work? How can we intervene to avoid becoming the bad boss?

Consider the following questions:

- Do you find yourself bored at work? Do you find the projects you are leading to be easy and no longer challenging?
- Do you find yourself less interested in studying the competition and market trends and continuing to learn and gain new skills?
- Do you find yourself going back to old bad habits you thought you had once kicked? Eating excessive amounts of sugar or caffeine, ordering take-out, or drinking more alcohol? Is there a void you may be trying to fill?
- Do you no longer participate in social events with colleagues?
- Do you find yourself canceling or finding excuses not to attend meetings, asking your team to just handle it?

(continued)

(*continued*)

- Did you once participate and share ideas, volunteer to lead initiatives, and now find that you would rather be under the radar at work?
- Do you spend most of your weekends sleeping, uninterested in leaving your house, or do you spend time with friends and family and focus on what you are passionate about?
- Do you struggle to get out of bed Monday mornings to head to work or to log onto your laptop? Are you still excited to be at your organization?

As you reflect on your answers, consider applying the framework shared previously on yourself. Can you proactively set up time with your leader? What would have to change for you to be excited about work again? Are you suffering from burnout that's leading to disengagement? (We will discuss burnout later on in the book.) Is it time to craft the exit plan to move on to what you are meant to do next?

Actively disengaged leaders can become bad bosses when their clear lack of interest in their own jobs, and growing resentment for the company, can negatively affect their teams. Their disengagement can infect the team, who may in turn lose interest in their work, especially if they don't have a boss there to coach and guide them. Team members may start to feel isolated and alone, driving them to make the decision to leave the company. Napping on the job from time to time might not seem like a big deal—or it may be a sign of something much bigger brewing. Watch out for the signs of disengagement in others and yourself to avoid becoming another bad boss wreaking havoc in our organizations.

Tips on Assessing Employee Engagement

■ Watch for signs of disengagement on your team.

■ Hold yourself accountable; don't ignore the signs and intervene quickly.

■ Apply the framework:

  ■ Be a mirror: reflect back the behaviors you are observing.

  ■ Allow space for them to reveal what's going on.

  ■ Ask them what has to change for them to be excited about work.

■ Spark their interest in learning again.

■ Create a plan for change and stick to it; disengaged employees may recommit to the organization or need to move on.

Watch for signs and self-reflect on your levels of engagement at work; consider how your disengagement can negatively impact your team.

4

The Boss Who Hovered Like a Helicopter and Enjoyed Redoing All of Our Work

After parting ways with the Napper, I went on to work for a few really good leaders. These good leaders helped me gain more confidence, coached me through mistakes, and pushed me to take on assignments I didn't think I was ready for. They temporarily restored my faith in our workplaces, as I began to experience firsthand that good leaders can and do exist.

In retrospect, I should have soaked up every single one of those good leader moments. I absolutely took them for granted, naive in thinking that I was done with bad bosses and now I was in "my good leader era." But once you have had a few really good leaders, the universe decides that you are due for a bad boss.

Enter the Chopper.

At this point in my career, most of my interactions with bad bosses were the ones who neglected you, didn't have time for you, forgot that you actually worked for them. Other than the Sheriff, who enjoyed targeting and bullying me, most of the bad bosses I had experienced and observed weren't present or interested in even being a boss. Their lack of availability was a driving force behind what made them so bad.

The Chopper was a newly promoted manager who came from the sales division. He managed a team with a handful of us in the office and some others who worked remotely. He always seemed to have his Clemson University coffee mug in hand. He would arrive early in the morning with his backpack slung across his shoulders and leave just in time to have dinner with his wife and girls. And whenever possible, he talked about his 10 minute commute into the office.

And here's what the Chopper was most known for: always being available.

Always around.

Always ready to give unsolicited feedback.

Always ready to dive into details that didn't concern him.

Always one of the first people to respond to group emails.

Always ready to do all of our jobs and not focus on his own.

He hovered like a helicopter. He strolled around on the floor, pausing for the occasional stop and chat. He would seem to move around in a pattern of concentric circles, going from one team member to another. He would have his phone in hand, emailing, texting, and calling those in other locations, and sometimes heading back to his desk. And then, he would magically reappear. He would suddenly land and settle in to help one of us. Even when we didn't ask for or need his help.

The Chopper had to approve every single task. Even if it was a $50 sales sample that he had approved verbally and in writing, he then had to manually approve it through the system and hit that button. Every single invoice had to have his name on it. Every single receipt he had to see. I had no power to even approve buying our agency partner a coffee.

The Chopper needed to be copied on every single email. "Please cc me" were the clear instructions from the first day I started working for him. He wanted to know every detail on every single project. He wanted to be kept "in the loop" at all times. He color-coded his emails, had dozens and dozens of folders lining his inbox, and used his draft folder as his to-do list. I agonized for hours sometimes over writing the simplest of emails, knowing he would read what I wrote and have an immediate response either contradicting what I wrote or asking more follow-up questions.

The Chopper was obsessed with receiving constant updates. While he was cc'd on emails, we had to provide detailed updates in our one-on-one weekly trackers, in our weekly team meeting agenda document, in our monthly team project milestone spreadsheet, and in the company's monthly update letter. I spent more time updating spreadsheets and trackers and docs, cutting and pasting the same information, than doing the actual work I was hired to do.

The Chopper would sometimes just message us "Hi." I would continue on with my work and just stare at the word "Hi." Sometimes I could see he was typing. Sometimes the "Hi" turned into a request, other times he just stopped typing, clearly distracted by another task. "Why can't he just tell us what he wants," a colleague complained to me at lunch one day. "I am so sick of that *hi*; just get to the point and tell me exactly what you want me to do."

The Chopper had a gift for overcomplicating the simplest of tasks. If we had to provide the latest sales data for this quarter's innovation, he would send an email with the request. Then he would gather us for a meeting to discuss the email. When we asked follow-up questions, he would provide contradictory answers.

He would then pull up his laptop and start pulling the data himself, while we all sat around and watched him for more than 30 minutes. This was just one of the many occasions where I watched him doing the work he had asked us to do.

And the Chopper wasn't a screamer or a yeller. For the most part, he always had a smile on his face at work. He genuinely seemed to enjoy and mastered the art of micromanaging all of us. Doing all of our jobs seemed to bring him so much more joy than doing his own job.

Before our annual June brand plan presentation, the Chopper's micromanaging tendencies were in full-blown effect. Almost every day for two weeks leading up to the presentation, we would sit at a circular table in the kitchen at 4 p.m. where he would pull up his laptop. I would watch him change the font to Times New Roman 12 to 14, and then usually back to 12. He would substitute random words for another. He would resize images. He would rewrite my sentences, with the revised version having the same exact meaning as my original work.

I watched the big black and white clock tick-tock away on the wall. I was in a perpetual state of panic, afraid I would miss the last train back into the city. And have to splurge on a very expensive Uber ride home.

On the day of our annual brand plan presentation, we all came in early to set up the conference room in preparation for senior management attending. He asked me to move all of the samples we had placed on the long table in front of each chair, from the top right to the bottom right. Before the meeting was about to start, I watched him slightly push in all the chairs and move the printed copies of the new campaign concept on the table down about an inch further. I also watched him rearrange the large vases we had filled with samples of our new products. He paced around the room, following us around and redoing what he had asked us to do until the presentation finally started.

One of my colleagues turned to me later and whispered, "What's the point of working on anything and putting time into it? The Chopper will just redo it anyway."

Unfortunately, the Chopper's smile and chipper mood was not enough to keep me motivated. Slowly, over time, he quietly killed my creative spirit. He killed any interest I had in taking initiative, going above and beyond, voicing my ideas, offering to help on other projects, and trying to make any decisions. He slowly but surely squeezed any joy I felt out of work.

While others resigned and moved on internally, I stayed and put my head down, doing my best to survive. Working for those other bad bosses had made me tolerant to a wide range of work trauma. And unbeknownst to me, I had even more bad bosses coming my way. So, I endured, thinking that was what I was supposed to do. After all, we can often convince ourselves that this bad boss isn't really as bad as they seem.

And I survived the Chopper. I was promoted about a year later. And I went on to manage a team for the first time. I was over the moon, and I was ready to be the very best boss I could be. Having experienced a handful of bad bosses, I was hopeful that I could be better because I knew what bad, very bad, and downright awful could look like.

A few months into my new assignment, we were working on a deck to present to management on our new cost-savings initiative. I was excited about all of the ideas we had come up with to save money for the division without sacrificing the quality of our products. I sent my feedback to the team in a timely manner; I didn't want them waiting on me.

In our meeting that afternoon, two team members pulled up the revisions I made to the deck and asked me the following questions:

- Can you help us understand why you revised the first slide?

- In the future, how should we think about which images to include or not?
- We noticed you revised the graph we included with different colors. Do you have a preference on which colors we use on future graphs?

These were the only ones I remembered. And there were a series of questions. Because they were thoughtfully and kindly telling me I was redoing their work, without any coaching, explanation, or reasoning. I was being a micromanager.

Had I suddenly become the Chopper?

That meeting that day was one of the biggest gifts my team could have ever given me: to help me avoid one of the many pitfalls of becoming a bad boss.

It was an important reminder for me that sometimes, without us even realizing it, bad habits from bad bosses can quietly be passed on to the next generation of leaders. Despite us proclaiming we will never become that bad boss, it can happen. So, it's up to us to watch for the signs and break those generational curses in our workplaces.

★★★★★

Years later, here's the question that I continue to ponder: Why can't some leaders stop micromanaging?

According to one global study taken during the pandemic, almost 50% of employees felt their bosses micromanaged them.[1] Another study cites that 73% of employees consider micromanagement one of the biggest red flags at work.[2] And 46% of employees say that micromanagement would be a reason for them to say, "I quit."[3] So many of us have experienced micromanagement firsthand; we know it can stop us from taking initiative and start to slowly erode trust on the team. We no longer feel valued. We can become disengaged and demotivated. Ultimately, being micromanaged can affect our performance.

Some of us may be labeled a "poor performer" and pushed out of the company.

Being micromanaged can be exhausting and lonely. If we do decide to confide in someone what's happening, the feedback, advice, and commentary can include the following:

- Your boss is just insecure, and they don't know what they are doing.
- We can learn something from everyone.
- You should tell them you don't like to be micromanaged.
- They just don't have the expertise or the experience to manage people.
- It is really about their need to be in control. Don't take it personally.
- Well, is there a reason they may be micromanaging you?
- Maybe it's not the worst thing. I have a boss who doesn't even know I exist!

Why Do We Micromanage?

As leaders, we can have our moments of getting deep into some of the details: getting involved in a tough client-facing project, intervening when tensions between colleagues escalate, assisting with a particularly difficult negotiation, or taking over a product launch not performing well in the market. However, micromanagement goes beyond just getting into details: it's a pattern of behavior that includes the excessive need to control aspects of how our teams work, the inability to delegate decisions, and often an obsession with gathering as much information as possible.

So why do some of us persistently micromanage versus others? Here are some reasons:

(continued)

(continued)

- We don't trust our teams to get all of the details right, the way we would.
- We know we have the expertise and can just get it done faster.
- We don't want to be embarrassed by any mistakes, so we need to triple-check everything.
- We miss doing our old jobs. We miss doing the research, pulling together the recommendation, and presenting the proposal.
- We aren't sure what else to work on. No one ever trained us or taught us on what we should be doing. What does it mean to manage anyway?

We will discuss more on why we behave this way and then learn how to tackle our micromanaging tendencies.

We talk a lot about micromanaging: the marketplace is filled with advice on how to work for a micromanager. What to do if you are being micromanaged, how to respond in the moment, and more. But why isn't there more guidance for those bosses who are the micromanagers? Why aren't we doing more to stop micromanagement in its tracks? Let's ask ourselves the following questions to assess if we are in fact a micromanager:

How Do I Know If I Am Micromanaging?

Sometimes, your team or colleagues may directly say that you are micromanaging. This may come up in employee engagement survey results, in performance review feedback, or in a live discussion. It may come up in employee exit interviews, so be sure to understand the reasons why people choose to leave.

Sometimes, they won't use the word *micromanaging*, like in the case of my former team giving me feedback. Here are some of the things they might say instead:

- Mita doesn't trust me to do the work I am leading and drive results.
- I have offered to implement tools to help Mita oversee our team's project workflow, and instead she wants to be cc'd on every single email.
- Mita doesn't have regular check-ins with me. Instead, we meet constantly but our time together is inefficient. I have a hard time concentrating on my work because she is always hovering.
- I can never actually make any decision on my own. Mita has to approve everything.
- Mita redoes most of my work. I'm unclear what I did wrong.

Persistent micromanagement can start to set little fires on your team and erode inclusion and trust. In employee engagement surveys, you may see a dip in team morale. You may also see an increase in self-reported burnout, loss of trust, and feeling a loss of control. Your team may be missing deadlines, may be less productive, unable to deliver high-quality work, and ultimately may walk out the door.

How Do I Understand Why I Might Be Micromanaging?

In my time coaching leaders, very few proclaim that they are a micromanager. As we discussed previously, to stop micromanaging, we must identify the root causes of micromanaging. What causes us to hover like helicopters?

Review the following statements. Be honest with yourself on what resonates:

- I feel a loss of control in my personal life, so I am finding ways to regain control at work, focusing on the details that I can directly affect and have ownership over.
- I have issues trusting people. It's hard for me to believe that someone can do the job as well as I can. I don't know how to hold people accountable or what to do if they make mistakes.
- I have trouble unplugging and enjoying my time off from work. I can't remember the last time I took a vacation and wasn't checking and responding to email or Slack. I get anxious when things are quiet and I don't know what's happening.
- I am scared because there aren't many people who look like me in leadership positions, and I constantly worry I will be next on the chopping block. I know I can prove my worth and value by knowing and being involved in every single detail of what my team is doing.
- I have too many things to do at work and at home. If I do it myself instead of delegating, it will be faster. It will take me too long to explain what needs to be done.
- I want to make sure I manage my leadership brand carefully. What people think of me and my team is really important. I can't afford for anyone to make a mistake.
- I actually really enjoying being in the details and doing the actual work. I don't enjoy coaching and directing people to do the work.
- I wasn't ready for this promotion they gave me. It was more money and a bigger title and so I went for it. But I actually don't know what to do.

When I reflected on these examples, I discovered the biggest reason I had been micromanaging was this: I was a boss for the first time. I was a new manager and I didn't know what to do.

The Biggest Mistake I Made as a First-time Manager: Micromanaging

According to the Center for Creative Leadership, more than 25% of first-time managers acknowledged that they were not ready to lead others to begin with.[4] And almost 60% of individuals said they never received training when they started their first leadership role. While Training Industry estimates that $166 billion is spent annually on leadership development in the United States, there remains a big opportunity to coach and support first-time managers.[5]

As a first-time manager, I couldn't make the leap from doing to directing. I obsessed over details that didn't matter but offered me some semblance of control. I micromanaged because I had unknowingly absorbed bad habits from the Chopper. I also micromanaged because I was scared to step into what I was meant to do, which was not to manage people, but to step up and coach and lead my team. Here's the advice I give first-time managers on how to avoid micromanaging and instead coach their teams.

Focus on the Output

In that first assignment leading a team, I recall telling my team to swap one image in a deck to another one that looked very similar. I asked my team to create more back-up slides for a five-minute presentation just in case we were asked "that question." I directed my team to rearrange the product samples on the table at a trade show. I didn't spend enough time focusing on the output.

Now, I focus on being aligned on the objective with the team. I ensure we have a clear understanding of what we want the end result to be. Are we trying to get approval for a new initiative? Are we trying to influence a leader to change vendors?

Or are we providing a monthly update on the state of the business?

If there's a company template to follow, we use that. If not, I let my team create a template and advise them on key elements. I let them know key questions I anticipate leadership asking. Finally, I coach them on ways to present the material in a way that's easy to understand with clear next steps.

Coach Through Mistakes

As a first-time manager, I was proud that I had a strong bias for action. I wanted to move quickly and make an impact as fast as possible. I would send back mistakes my team had made, already fixed for them to easily incorporate: rewriting sentences, redoing calculations, reformatting tables. I thought I was doing all of us a favor, working quickly so we could move onto the next thing. I was also pitching in and helping; I wasn't asking them to redo anything. But by correcting their mistakes, I wasn't teaching them anything.

Don't fix the mistakes. Coach through the mistakes. You should discuss live with your team areas of opportunities, why something wasn't correct, not positioned appropriately, or was a calculation error. Work through the mistake with them. Show them other options if there's not one right answer. Have them correct the mistake. If the project is already complete, remind them of how they can apply this lesson on a future initiative.

Finally, Don't Be a Helicopter Manager

I knew managing people for the first time was a privilege, and that I was responsible for helping them grow in their careers. And while I had positive intent and I cared deeply for them, the impact was that I became a helicopter manager. Similar to a helicopter parent, I was always hovering and nearby. I was ready to fight any battle for them at work; if someone argued with them or asked for something last minute, I was right there to intervene. I was ready to jump in and help with an initiative without giving them the time and space to tackle it themselves. I was overly responsive to group emails, responding right away without giving my team a chance to answer. I thought I was being helpful.

Give your teams the space to take initiative, to drive and own their work, to test and try things, and to also fail. Clap loudly and proudly for them when they do well. Have their backs and provide air cover when they fail. Allow them to grow as individuals. Remember that you are not a first-time manager: you are a first-time leader. Your job is not to micromanage people. Your job is to step up to coach and lead.

How Does One Stop Micromanaging?

As leaders, we must understand the difference between micromanaging and coaching. When we micromanage, we tell our teams exactly how to do their work, monitor how the work is being done, and we may end up doing the work for them. When we coach, we spend time explaining our expectations for inputs and outputs, teach them the skills they need to complete the task at hand, coach them through mistakes, and empower them to make an impact and reach their potential at work.

Refer to these questions to monitor your micromanaging tendencies:

- Why do I want to redo the work my team submitted? Is it factually inaccurate? Is it not presented in a clear and concise manner? Does it not meet the objectives we set out?
- Why do I need to make this decision? What happens if someone else on this team makes the decision?
- Why do I need to know where my team is and monitor their working hours? Has something happened to make me lose trust in their ability to complete the work?

- What details matter and what details don't matter? Have I communicated this to my team?
- What work can I delegate? What work am I holding onto and need to let go of?
- Why do I set up impromptu meetings and consistently check in on my team? Have I considered scheduling regular check-ins where we can review key project milestones?
- Do I consistently ask for feedback on my team on what I can do differently? To make sure I am not hovering, and I am in coach mode?
- Have I asked my boss for help in training, guidance, and support on how to get better at leading teams?
- Finally, am I excited to manage and coach people, or have I been pressured into leading teams? Would I be happier building my expertise as an individual contributor?

Micromanaging over time can destroy our cultures. It's the small ways in which we hover over teams, do their work for them, and our inability to coach and teach that can set little fires in the organization. Teams become demotivated and stop contributing ideas. They can't make decisions on their own or do meaningful work because they have been trained that their boss will tell them exactly what to do. So don't become that bad boss who hovers like a helicopter. Don't spend the time you have available squeezing the joy out of work and breaking trust and inclusion on your teams. Spend that time you have available to help your teams do their very best work.

Tips on Stopping Micromanagement in Its Tracks

- Start by understanding the difference between micromanaging and coaching.
- Ask the following key questions to assess if you are currently in micromanaging mode:
  - How do I know if I am micromanaging?
  - How do I understand why I might be micromanaging?
  - How does one stop micromanaging?
- Remember, avoid micromanaging mistakes first-time managers make by doing the following:
  - Focus on the output.
  - Coach through mistakes.
  - Steer clear of being a helicopter manager.
- Proactively reach out to your team to ensure you are not micromanaging and are staying in coach mode.

5

The Boss Who Cried Wolf, Because Everything Was Urgent

As I progressed in my career, the ghost of the Chopper stayed with me. I continued to have the internal battle of monitoring my hovering tendencies, stopping myself from becoming overly involved in details that just didn't matter. I moved to the next phase of my career from not only having a helicopter hovering over me but also to now constantly being in fire drill mode. It was like working in a building where the piercing sounds of fire alarms never stopped going off. With the faint clouds of smoke always lurking in the back.

Enter the White Rabbit. Or WR, as we affectionately called her.

The White Rabbit appears on screen in Disney's *Alice in Wonderland* singing, "Oh, my fur and whiskers! I'm late, I'm late, I'm late!" He scurries around Alice. "I'm late, I'm late! For a very important date! No time to say 'hello, goodbye,' I'm late, I'm late, I'm late!"[1]

He holds onto a very oversized clock and runs around in a tizzy concerned he may be late for the royal garden party. And that the Queen of Hearts may see him come in late and exclaim, "Off with his head!"

Our White Rabbit rushed into work every morning with her oversized, worn-down brown Marc Jacobs tote, racing straight toward her desk. She always appeared to be late for something, on her phone loudly, sometimes on speaker, hurrying around the floor. On most mornings we would watch some team member scurrying behind her. Likely they had found her in the hallway, hoping to catch just five minutes with her. She was very good at sending urgent emails and yet she wasn't very good at responding back, after we had quickly sent what she needed or had a follow-up question. She had moved onto the next fire drill, the next chaotic, unexpected situation that needed her immediate and complete attention. Fire drills that she had usually created herself.

WR loved typing her emails with the subject lines in all capital letters in those urgent moments, with hardly anyone included in the CC line, but up to a dozen people or more at a time in the "To line":

"URGENT REQUEST"

"NEEDS IMMEDIATE ATTENTION"

"PLEASE RESPOND ASAP"

"INPUTS REQUIRED BY EOD"

"MEET AT 12 P.M. FOR A TEAM HUDDLE"

Like my former boss the Devil, WR also forwarded many emails with little context, except to change the subject line to a fire drill headline to capture our attention.

WR enjoyed telling people how "slammed" she was. "So busy" and "in back-to-backs" and "fighting fires" and "in the trenches" and "getting called into urgent meetings by management."

If you weren't convinced that she was busy with fire drills, she would throw in the "didn't even have time to go to the bathroom yet today" for good measure.

WR's fire drills came in many forms. She called urgent team huddles that weren't urgent at all. She sat on leadership requests that came in weeks prior, forgetting to send them. This created another fire drill, giving us now only 24 hours to complete the task. She would get wind of a potential customer meeting happening in a week and ask us to pull data immediately. And then the meeting never happened or was pushed out by months. She had us not once, but twice, started a new monthly report no one asked her to start. She had us scramble to pull it together to try and impress leadership. Those reports only lasted two months until she moved onto the next urgent issue at hand.

Every fire drill she created had one inevitable outcome: we would have to drop everything, immediately stop what we were doing. It reminded me of what I once learned in the first grade when a firefighter came in: "Stop, drop, and roll" if your clothing ever catches on fire. This felt like a daily occurrence at work. In the end, we took our time and energy away from work that was making real impact. We rushed with speed to stop, drop, and roll for whatever fire drill she had decided to create that day.

As someone now managing a team, I tried to filter the WR fire drills and shield my direct reports as much as I could. I had to stop myself from gossiping about WR with the team; many of them couldn't stand her. They didn't understand how she was given the responsibility of leading such a large team. I tried to defend her half-heartedly by saying things like "Don't worry, I'll handle it" and "She must have just forgotten" and "I'll get an extension."

I dealt with many of the fire drills myself, attempting to manage up to her. I became better at deciphering her requests, asking follow-up questions, and proposing alternative solutions:

- "Could this wait until next week?"
- "Instead of slides, I sent you a paragraph on the recent campaign results you can forward to leadership."
- "We filled this form out last month; here it is attached again."
- "I can get this data to you on Wednesday."
- "If you want the team to start working on this request, we will have to stop working on the other request you sent this morning."

I would receive any of the following responses from WR:

- "Okay."
- "Let's talk live" (which meant spending time, sometimes hours, trying to track her down).
- No response (most likely outcome).

Unlike the Chopper, who micromanaged yet surprisingly moved pretty quickly when it came to pushing work along, WR was a bottleneck. She was overwhelmed with the number of fire drills she created, clogging the entire system. She got stuck, couldn't move forward, give direction, or make decisions. We missed deadlines because she was busy inventing issues. And then more fire drills magically appeared to explain why we missed those deadlines in the first place.

"She's no longer the White Rabbit, she's the boss who cried wolf," exclaimed my colleague, Jennifer. "Everything is urgent and nothing is urgent. What a raging dumpster fire."

My colleague was right. With every fire drill WR started, more gasoline was thrown onto the fire as it grew, the flames growing higher and higher. And the more overwhelmed WR got, the worse her behavior became.

WR started texting me at 6 a.m. for inputs she needed for a weekly 8 a.m. management meeting. She would forget the meeting was happening and inevitably text in a panic. When I wouldn't respond, she would call every 10 minutes or so to try and get my attention. If I didn't respond, she would start calling my team members, who would then start texting me.

WR started finding us on those rare days that we decided not to eat lunch at our desks. And invent a reason for us to come back with her to our desks for something she needed. She would brag about how busy she was and that she didn't have time to eat lunch.

WR's behavior reached an all-time low on one Friday in June. We had summer hours, which meant we could stop work at 12 p.m. And if you worked for WR, you were lucky if you got any summer Fridays off. About 12 p.m. on that Friday, WR realized we did indeed have a real deadline she forgot about; we had to update a deck by 5 p.m. This deck was for the CEO.

She sent an urgent email: MEET NOW FOR A TEAM HUDDLE.

Only four people, including her, walked into the conference room.

"Where is everybody?" she asked, looking around confused.

Christian took a summer Friday and had just walked out.

Supriya just sat at her desk, pretending she didn't see the email.

Tessa had been calling in sick for several weeks now, once a week.

Ali was on vacation, and this time he wasn't checking email while he was away.

Phil was at lunch in the cafeteria, enjoying his personal pepperoni pan pizza.

WR was crying wolf. And most of the team had stopped listening. She had lost the ability to gather us for a real crisis.

The four of us sat around the table, each tackling different slides to update. And then 60 minutes later, we were still working. I started to gather my stuff as WR watched me get up from the table.

"My parents are coming into town. I need to get home."

She stared at me and waited, not saying a word. Probably waiting for me to change my mind. And this time, I wasn't going to. I walked out of the conference room and went to spend the weekend with my parents and my husband.

On that following Monday, back at work, the team was in the kitchen buzzing about what had happened over lattes and cappuccinos: On Friday, after I left, WR remembered she had a chiropractor appointment she couldn't reschedule at 3 p.m. She asked Jessie on the team to go with her to the appointment, sit in the waiting room, and work on the deck while WR was with her chiropractor. Then, she asked Jessie to come back to her house to finish the deck. And sent Jessie home about 7 p.m. in a very long and expensive Friday night Uber back to Manhattan. Jessie, being one of the newer managers on the team, obliged and went ahead with WR. I didn't blame Jessie; a younger version of myself would have probably made the same choice.

"That's awful," I blurted out. I couldn't control my reaction in front of the team. "I can't believe she did that."

WR, like many a bad boss, was protected by the higher-ups. In her case, it was by one senior leader who had been there for quite some time. When a company restructuring happened, I was rotated to another team. And WR stayed right where she was, creating endless fire drills, while more people left her team over the months to come. When that senior leader who protected her finally retired, WR's power and false sense of credibility diminished quickly. She was assigned a special projects role and became an internal consultant, with no team reporting into her. Now it would seem that she had no one else but herself to help her extinguish the fires she kept setting.

★★★★★

So why do we create a false sense of urgency in our workplaces?

Over the years in coaching leaders, I have heard some of the following rationale:

- "We are running low on cash and not sure how much longer we can make payroll. So yes, everything is urgent. It's wartime."
- "We need to create a sense of urgency to help boost productivity."
- "We set fake deadlines and quick turnaround times to ensure the work gets done."
- "We must make sure leadership knows what we are working on. There are more layoffs coming and we need to stay relevant."
- "We don't have time to plan; there's just too much going on. So, we need our teams to just get stuff done and stop whining about the workload."

Constantly living in a false state of urgency can have significant impact on productivity. While some leaders create a culture of false urgency to drive results, it can have in fact the opposite effect. Throughout the course of my career, I have witnessed firsthand how bad bosses like the White Rabbit, the boss who cried wolf, and the boss who "runs around like a chicken with its head cut off" can slowly chip away at their teams. When we work on a team where everything is urgent, we can live in a chronic state of being overwhelmed. We can miss deadlines. We don't understand what the difference between important or urgent is. We can rush and deliver a poorer quality work product. We start to distrust what our boss says, moving from one fire drill to another, where nothing seems to be solved, and it seems like all smoke and mirrors. We don't feel anything we are contributing actually matters on our team. The constant fire drills can lead to stress, anxiety, and exhaustion. In some cases, it leads to burnout.

According to a HubSpot report, lost productivity can cost companies $1.8 trillion a year.[2] Bad bosses like the Devil, who never made time for us; the Sheriff, who was a bully; the Napper, who was sleeping on the job and completely disengaged; the Chopper, who did our jobs for us; the White Rabbit, who convinced us everything was urgent—all ultimately break inclusion and trust on teams. When we feel like our contributions don't matter, that our voice doesn't matter, and that we don't matter at work, productivity will take a nosedive. No new system, no new process, no new policy can check the box and fix this bad boss behavior. Only holding each other, and ourselves, accountable from becoming these bad bosses will start to change our work cultures.

Over the years, as I have thought about the motivations of my former boss, the White Rabbit, I came to this conclusion: she assigned urgency to everything she did because she believed that would make her look more successful. Being busy, running around, and always being in perpetual fire drill mode was a status symbol for her. She wore that badge loudly and proudly. Creating fire drills helped boost and build her busy leadership persona and endeared her to leadership—or at least one key member of leadership. She was one of their firefighters. And she was busy putting out the fires she had intentionally set to show how valuable she was. It gave her a sense of purpose. It gave her instant gratification. Busy was her form of social currency and how she derived power at work. And maybe, her constantly being so busy was also tied to her sense of self-worth.

Why Are You in Constant Fire Drill Mode?

Before we discuss how we can stop creating a false sense of urgency in our workplaces, we need to understand why we are in constant fire drill mode. Do we, knowingly or unknowingly, thrive in the chaos at work? Consider the following questions and self-reflect:

- When you think of your childhood, would you describe it as chaotic or calm?
- If it was chaotic, do you see a pattern of being drawn to chaotic relationships and work environments as an adult?
- Are you more comfortable in chaos than in stable work environments?
- Do you find yourself feeling comforted when you are constantly in busy mode?
- Do you think creating a sense of urgency shows your value as a leader?
- How do you measure your productivity at work? Is it tied to how many meetings you are in, how many emails you send, and what you check off your to-do list at the end of the day?
- Do you glorify busyness as a leader? Do you brag to your team about being in back-to-back meetings and not having the time to take a break, eat lunch, or go to the bathroom?

(continued)

(continued)

- Do you think your team members who are not busy enough are lazy or just not committed to their jobs?
- Do you value team members who display an intense sense of urgency more than those who are calm and collected?

For some of us, working in an environment in chaos, turmoil, and in constant fire drill mode may actually be easier. We don't know or understand what productivity looks like, and so we think productivity is interchangeable with "urgency" or "very busy." We may operate like this at work due to experiences from our childhood or because we reported into a bad boss like the White Rabbit or for other reasons we have yet to discover. Once we can identify the cause of our bad boss behavior, and watch for potential signs, we can stop creating a false sense of urgency on our teams.

Most of us will never exhibit all the extreme behaviors of the White Rabbit. And each of us, under the right circumstances, can find ourselves creating or perpetuating a false sense of urgency on our teams. Here's a simple framework I follow to ensure that not everything is always urgent.

Start by Defining What Is Urgent

Ensure that you and your team have a clear understanding of what urgent means. If something is urgent, it's time sensitive, critical, and requires immediate attention or action. It may be a request from the CEO, a customer, or an investor who needs some of the team, or all of the team, to help.

And if it's truly urgent, there will likely be a negative impact to the business if the situation is not addressed swiftly.

Fake fire drills and a false sense of urgency seem critical in the moment but aren't actually imperative to moving the business forward. Like in the case of my former boss, she continued to be rewarded and supported by leadership for a myriad of reactive behaviors, including fake and aggressive deadlines, an extremely meeting-heavy culture with last-minute ad hoc team huddles, and constant urgent requests due ASAP. Her behavior stopped us from doing thoughtful and meaningful work.

So now when I have identified something to be urgent, I do the following:

- Pause one more time and ask myself if this is truly urgent. Can this wait? What happens if this doesn't get done today or within the next 48 hours? It's a reminder to not become the boss who cries wolf and makes everything urgent.
- Be clear on why this is urgent, what the deliverable is, who is asking for it and by when.
- Stick to the one mode of communicating an urgent request that you have agreed to as a team, marking it urgent in an email or a Slack; if I need to gather team members immediately (e.g., restructuring, resignation, funding cut), only then do I call their cell directly.
- Identify and assign who should help and why, instead of including the entire team and having them figure it out.
- Pitch in to help where I can, without micromanaging or duplicating any efforts; offer to review the final product before the deadline.

Once you start defining what is urgent, then you can move forward to helping your team prioritize on a regular basis.

Help Your Team Prioritize and Reprioritize

When I think of my time working for the Chopper and the White Rabbit, they shared some bad boss behaviors, but the biggest similarity was this: the inability to prioritize. With the Chopper, we met all the time because he wanted to know everything we were working on, and with the White Rabbit, we met all the time but in a complete frenzy. We were always caught in a reactive state versus being proactive about the work that would be coming our way.

So when it comes to helping teams prioritize, here's what I focus on:

- Be sure to review, prioritize, and reprioritize regularly individual and team initiatives; have this documented in one place, and not multiple places, which can create more chaos and duplicative work.
- Ask yourself the following questions when prioritizing as a team:
  - Start with the long view and work backwards. Don't overly focus on the tasks with the shortest deadlines.
    - What projects need to be finished by this quarter? By the end of the month? By the end of the week?
  - What has changed? Are there new obstacles? Has funding been cut? Do we have more resourcing than anticipated?
  - What projects should we put on pause? When would we resume this and why?
  - What projects should we stop completely? Is ego or personal agenda getting in the way of walking away from this work that's no longer relevant?
- Invite and allow your team to challenge what's urgent and reprioritize together.

- Create the time and space to have planning sessions so you can map out and prioritize the work on a quarterly basis.
- Don't reward or encourage reactive behavior from team members. This will only train the team to start viewing everything as urgent and just get the job done any way they can.
- Do reward team members who plan and prepare, invest time in understanding the problem up front, who are thoughtful about their approach, and push you and the team to discern what is urgent and what is not.

Remember, our job as leaders is to prioritize and to avoid creating a false sense of urgency. It's our job to step back and help the team remember and focus on what's important for the business.

Protect Your Team from Fake Fire Drills

Once you define what is urgent and help your team prioritize, you must protect your team from the external requests that will come from your boss, other leaders, cross-functional team members, customers, vendors, and more that will be marked as urgent. Some of them will need your immediate attention; others will be fake fire drills.

Ask yourself the following when it comes to how you protect your team's time and avoid potentially fake fire drills:

- Do you automatically say yes to anything your boss asks you to do, assuming the team will just figure it out?
- Do you have a hard time pushing back on incoming requests because you are worried it will negatively affect how others view you as a leader?

- Do you struggle with deciding what's important for the team to work on?
- Do you expect your team to say yes to everything they are approached to work on?
- Do you ask your team to check with you before committing to do more work?

When responding to urgent requests, we may be worried that if we push back, we may be letting others down, be labeled as an ineffective leader who isn't committed or isn't a team player, or worse, put our job or our team's jobs in jeopardy. And part of our job as leaders is to navigate these tough conversations and stand up for our teams and protect their time.

Here are some ways to approach and vet what requests are actually urgent. Consider the following language to adapt to your specific situation:

- "Thanks for sending this request along. Due to other priorities, we can't deliver this tomorrow and can deliver it next week. I appreciate your understanding."
- "It would be great to have the context to understand what's driving this sense of urgency. We can get you the first part of this request in a week's time, and the second part of the request in two weeks."
- "Happy to work on this. Can we discuss the other two urgent tasks that were sent to our team yesterday? Which of these is the most important?"
- "We have reviewed as a team our priorities and we are juggling a lot as we head toward the end of the quarter. Could we get on a quick call to discuss? I would love your guidance."
- "My boss told me this week that this project was canceled. Let me connect with her first. If you have any additional information to share that would be helpful."

Fire drills will happen. Chaos will occur. Urgent, important, and "requires immediate attention" issues will come up in our workplaces. And when we make everything an urgent, very important, must drop all things and tend to fire drill, we create a team culture where innovation and creativity are squashed, and individuals stop contributing in meaningful and impactful ways. Don't become that bad boss who runs around exclaiming everything is urgent and creating the perpetual feeling that as a team you are never on time, but always running behind. Do be the leader who roots out that false sense of urgency from their teams and gives them the time and the space to thrive.

Tips on Preventing a Fire Drill Culture

- Start by understanding why you may be in constant fire drill mode. Identify what is driving your behavior before jumping into an action plan.
- Define what is urgent; have a clear understanding with your team on what urgent means and how your team comes together to tackle these issues.
- Help your team prioritize; be open to your team challenging you on projects that are no longer a priority.
- Protect your team from fake fire drills:
  - Reflect on how you protect your team's time or how you allow your team to be robbed of their time.
  - Adopt language that positions you as a collaborative leader when approached about fire drills; seek to understand the context of why something is urgent before jumping in to say yes to everything.

6

The Boss Who Ruled with Fear, Perched on Her Throne, Clutching Tightly to Her Crown

"Why the hell is the font on this package luxe lemon yellow?!"

Up until this point in my career, I had never worked for someone who screamed at me.

This wasn't her just raising her voice. Not speaking very loudly. Not a shout. Not an occasional loud outburst. She screamed and she yelled. You could hear her from her office, hear her from down the hall, across the floor, and sometimes through the elevators as you were coming up to the building.

My parents, my brother, my husband, my friends . . . I couldn't recall any adult in my life who had ever screamed at me. Ever.

Until I worked for Medusa.

And Medusa just happened to wear Chanel. And she wore lots of it.

Before I met Medusa, I was in my good boss—I mean great leader—era. I had moved on from the White Rabbit and soon after found my next really, really good boss. I worked for a vice president who promoted me, coached me, guided me, had my back, and just let me soar. He was an incredible leader. I learned so much from him about the beauty industry and how to be a better storyteller. In fact, I have tried over the years to find him to send a note of gratitude. To let him know he set the standard high for me on how a good boss and good leader should be. So, at the time, going to work for Medusa, who was doused in Chanel No. 5, felt like one of the biggest career crashes of all time.

I remember that moment when I was summoned into an empty office, where my then vice president and senior director told me I would be moved off my current team to go and work for the Medusa. I was in disbelief. I was being punished for being a high performer and going to work for a toxic leader whose business was in double-digit decline. I had to move over as an individual contributor for the time being and try to rebuild the team.

I was able to somehow mutter, "She's really not an inclusive leader. I don't see myself thriving on her team." The senior director smiled at me sympathetically; he had told me himself once what a toxic bully she was. The vice president, however, was not pleased with my candid feedback.

Somehow, even though she was a well-known toxic bully, I was the one now in trouble for speaking up. I was immediately branded a troublemaker, a pot stirrer, a poor performer, a detractor, and someone who wasn't a team player. A colleague in human resources (HR) had said to me, "Why would you say anything? We all know she's an issue. You ruined your chances of a promotion this year."

So, for 13 months, I reported into Medusa who wore Chanel.

She screamed at us about why eyeshadow sales samples were late (because she decided to order them last minute).

She screamed at us about why we ordered the house salad instead of the Caesar salad for our lunch meeting (because the restaurant ran out of the Caesar salad).

She screamed at us about not having her Chanel shoes with her when she was about to present to the board. I'll never forget the relay race my colleagues and I did to get those Chanel shoes from our office to where the board meeting was taking place. Ten long Manhattan blocks away.

She would openly mock coworkers and make fun of "their accent." She asked me a few times how I had managed to get rid of my accent. How did I learn to speak English so well?

She would tell us we were stupid and slow to our faces.

She would not only scream but also curse in meetings and point her fingers. It's the first time I heard a boss drop so many f-bombs. Her white face would turn bright red. Occasionally she tossed a pen across the room. I watched people run into conference rooms to disappear, or slink back in their chairs, or go around corners to hide from her wrath.

She would monitor when we came in through her glass office, when and how long we took lunch breaks, and point out our lack of worth ethic when we left "early" at 8 p.m.

She once shouted at the team to hurry and line the mascara samples up "like good little Black soldiers" before the president walked in.

She complained that our Indian lunch we had ordered was too smelly, told me my clothing was "basic," and I lacked fashion sense (ironically, my job didn't pay me enough to buy Chanel).

She asked me why "you people" always have "hard-to-pronounce names."

Finally, she also wasn't very good at her job. In fact, she was terrible at what she was actually hired to do. We wrote her emails, pulled all of the data, created her decks, gave her detailed talking points, worked with vendors to create sales videos, set up the conference rooms with elaborate props and samples when she was asked to present all of our work to the president.

It was during preparation for one of those meetings that she even hurled one of those Chanel shoes at my colleague. (I was so traumatized by this incident that I had buried this memory away. My husband had to remind me of it. I guess he does listen to all of my stories after all.)

Medusa's reputation for being a toxic, terrible, and terrifying leader was well known across the organization. She had joined us from another beauty company; others who had once worked with her would later reach out to share their horrible experiences in my LinkedIn inbox. Her nickname was given to her long before I met her. After one year of leading one team at our organization, the entire team of 15 people that she inherited all left. She was then moved to lead another team, the team I was forced to join. After one year of leading that team, again, another dozen people who worked for her left the company. Including me.

Medusa drove strong results from me in the short term. I was terrified of being in the path of her wrath, so I worked overtime to deliver things on time, and sometimes in advance, before she even asked. I was in early at 7 a.m. some mornings (this was before I had children) and would stay late into the evening, pulling 12-hour days. I was afraid of being fired.

And then, despite having a wide range of bad bosses, working for Medusa hit me hard. I couldn't keep up with the pace.

I was constantly worried about making mistakes, not working fast enough, being yelled at, or retaliated against. I couldn't think clearly. And when I did have an idea on how to do something a different way, I just didn't. I kept my head down and kept working. And with the little energy I had, my husband and close friends convinced me to start looking externally. I started my first of many "get-out" spreadsheets tracking the over 40 companies I interviewed with in one of the toughest financial markets that year. Because I had to do just that—get out.

Two of my coworkers, Adam and Hugh, who were on another team, were infuriated and in absolute disbelief at what was happening.

"What did she do today?" Adam would run over from the other side of the floor to my desk when he saw the coast was clear. "Why don't we all just stage an intervention and march into that glass office of hers? I will organize it. Or how about I go talk to HR? Or we can . . ."

"No, that's not going to help, but thank you for asking," I would whisper quietly, while sipping my lukewarm Earl Grey tea. I was grateful for their friendship and support, and knew any intervention would only make things worse. If that was even possible.

Adam and Hugh would drag me out to lunch with them at least once a week. We would sit sipping the most delicious vegetable udon noodle soup at a tiny place around the corner. I would slurp the soup as quickly as possible, watching for my phone to light up with Medusa messages.

"How does Medusa continue to have a job here? After everything she has done?" Adam asked, shaking his head, and then snatching my phone away and encouraging me to eat for 10 minutes in peace.

"It's because she's Greta's pit bull, she does all the dirty work that Greta doesn't want to know about," Hugh said. "Greta knows how horrible Medusa is; they all know and they just don't care," Hugh continued on. "Greta will keep Medusa around as long as they both are here."

Adam and Hugh would alternate bringing me tea and treats. They would message me to check in, send me funny memes, threaten to leave a Medusa sculpture head in her office, offer to report her to HR, send me job listings, intercept when they saw her to distract her from having another explosion, and offer to be references. And 13 months later, I finally got out.

In my last two weeks at that organization, Greta, the division president, HR, and other leaders relentlessly hounded me to give the real reason why I was leaving. But I wouldn't say the truth aloud. I stuck to the story I had crafted, to my key talking points: "I am leaving for a better opportunity."

When I finally escaped, my commute went from 25 minutes, back to another 90 minutes each way (on a good day, depending on the temperament of New Jersey Transit). At that point, I would have quadrupled my commute time to escape the wrath of Medusa. I would have commuted from Manhattan to Boston and back every day just to be away from her.

Once I left Medusa, I never looked back. I had no interest in knowing if she and Greta were still there. I didn't quietly stalk her on social media, I didn't block her number, I didn't keep in touch with any of the other team members, except for Adam and Hugh.

Two years later, I received a call from a recruiter for an exciting opportunity. When I asked who had recommended me, they said Medusa. They were talking to her about leading the group. My throat went dry. I thanked him for his time and said I would be passing on the opportunity.

It was only recently I confessed to a friend that I can't stand the smell of Chanel No. 5. Some memories take a long time to fade.

★★★★★

To this day, Medusa is still one of the top three bad bosses I have ever had in my career.

She ruled with fear. She used fear as a tactic to drive results. She used fear as a tactic to intimidate and to hold onto her power and her status. She used fear to make herself feel significant. She also used fear as a tactic to keep her distance from us, so we wouldn't discover how scared and insecure she actually was.

In my time coaching leaders, I have heard a myriad of excuses to justify, excuse, tolerate, enable, and ultimately support fear-based leadership:

"She is just under some stress. This too shall pass."

"It is good to be scared. Gets the adrenaline going."

"We need to drive results. We don't have time to deal with people who are easily offended."

"My boss was also a yeller. Helped me get thicker skin!"

"Let's just get through these next two quarters. We just can't make any leadership changes now."

Some leaders still haven't come to grips with what fear-based leadership is actually costing their organizations.

Why Do We Lead with Fear?

Most of us will never become the Medusa who wore too much Chanel. We won't ever go to that extreme of leading with fear and throwing our shoe at a team member. And under the right circumstances, we may be inclined to, drawn to, or even persuaded by our own bosses to be the boss who is feared. Consider the following questions:

■ How many of the bosses whom you have worked for were you afraid of? What made you afraid of them?

(continued)

(*continued*)

- Did you enjoy working for these bosses who scared you? Did they get the best out of you at work?
- Do you remember specific fear-based tactics your bosses used? Do you find yourself using those same tactics now?
- Does your current boss encourage you to use fear-based leadership?
- Do you find yourself able to think clearly in your moments of anger or when you are lashing out at your team? As you look back at those moments, do you think you were logical, reasonable, or rational?
- Do you believe making your team fearful of you drives better results?
- Do you think intimidating and scaring them when the business is struggling is the best way to motivate them?
- Do you find yourself threatened by the high performers on your team? Are you worried that one of them could replace you?
- Are you envious of peers who don't lead with fear, and are well liked and respected?

When we lead with fear, we may be trying to cover up our own fears. We haven't dealt with what we are afraid of. We are afraid of not being included, we are afraid that we aren't smart enough or good enough, we are afraid that we don't know what we are doing, we are afraid of failing, we are afraid of being criticized.

Our fears stop us from reaching our potential. Our fears then also stop us from letting our teams reach their potential. If we understand the root cause of what is driving our fears, we can stop the fear from reoccurring. Facing our fears head on can also help shake off insecurities and continue to build our confidence as leaders.

More than one-third of leaders in US companies lead through fear.[1] Creating workplace cultures based on fear costs the economy approximately $36 billion each year in lost productivity.[2] Nearly 40% of fear-based leaders said, "they strongly believe that stress can be positively harnessed."[3]

And yet, here are two other observations fear-based leaders have also had of their teams:

- 90% witnessed a decline in team members' productivity.[4]
- 60% acknowledged their "direct reports are unhappy with their job."[5]

When you lead with fear on your teams, here are the consequences. Here's the detrimental impact of fear in our workplaces:

- **Fear kills communication.** Individuals stop speaking up in fear of punishment or retaliation. Because they move to survival mode in fear of losing their jobs, they don't want to say anything or do anything that could jeopardize their employment.
- **Fear leads to decreased productivity.** When individuals are being screamed at, threatened, intimidated, berated, humiliated, and more, how can they be expected to do their best work? They begin to live in a perpetual state of fear at work.
- **Fear isolates team members.** Fear can divide and conquer a team. Each individual on the team is trying to survive each day. Because they don't trust their boss, they might also lose trust in other team members. In other cases, it can bond team members against a common enemy. (We will talk later on about how bad bosses can actually bring team members together.)

- **Fear kills creativity and innovation.** Individuals might not be thinking clearly, their thoughts clouded. They are afraid to try new things and take risks. What if they make a mistake? What if they make the wrong decision? They are less likely to create new ideas and solutions. Fear promotes sticking to the status quo.
- **Fear leads to burnout.** As we have discussed throughout the book, all of these bad boss behaviors can ultimately lead to burnout, including a boss who is only available at midnight, a boss who bullies, a disengaged boss, a boss who is a micromanager, and a boss who creates fake fire drills. Fear creates a stressful and chaotic work environment, slowly chipping away at an individual's confidence and capabilities in themselves to deliver great work, leading to burnout.

If you have someone like Medusa on your team, they are probably the worst-kept secret in the organization. In other cases, the fear-based leadership may be more subtle and the signs harder to find. Here are three questions to consider.

Why Are We Suddenly Labeling Team Members as Detractors?

As soon as I and others spoke out about our bad boss, we were labeled as troublemakers. Pot stirrers. Detractors. For two years in a row, I had received the highest performance rating possible, and then suddenly, I became the problem for speaking up. I was the detractor, accused of criticizing my bad boss and the company unfairly.

Many organizations use Net Promoter Score (NPS), a marketing metric calculated from a survey, asking individuals questions to determine how likely they are to recommend a product or service to someone else in their life.[6] Detractors are labeled unhappy customers based on their NPS results. They are unhappy with the products or service, they likely won't buy it again, and they may even speak badly about their experience to others. In most cases, leaders will scramble to quickly resolve the issue and try to make that customer happy again.

As I have often said, our employees are our forgotten customers. In the case of a customer who is unhappy with a product or service, we will jump through hoops to win back their loyalty. An employee raises a concern, and we may immediately label them a detractor. Rather than trying to make them happy again, we may plot to push them out. As we discussed previously, start by believing employees' experiences. Seek to understand and learn more about what's happening. Labeling someone a detractor is a lazy way of putting blame on the employee. And ultimately not wanting to understand the situation and accept the truth: there are people on your team being terrorized by an abusive boss.

How Can I Spot Signs of Burnout?

If your team is trapped in a perpetual state of fear, burnout may be waiting for them just around the corner. Or burnout may have already arrived. According to the World Health Organization, "Burn-out is a syndrome conceptualized as resulting from chronic workplace stress that has not been successfully managed."[7] Burnout can be characterized as[8]

- Feelings of energy depletion or exhaustion
- Increased mental distance from one's job, or feelings of negativism or cynicism related to one's job
- Reduced professional efficacy

According to Gallup, here are some signs that your team may be suffering from burnout:[9]

- Burned-out employees are "63% more likely to take a sick day."
- They are "2.6 times as likely to be actively seeking a different job."
- They are "half as likely to discuss how to approach their performance goals with their manager."
- They are "13% less confident in their performance."

Other signs can include disengagement, when they stop participating in meetings, don't respond to emails or Slack, and don't want to take on new work. They can also isolate themselves, react with defensiveness or other emotion when receiving feedback, and produce lower-quality work.

How you lead, and how you expect others to lead on your team, is one of the most important ways to prevent and mitigate burnout.

Are You Suffering from Burnout?

As leaders, we can also suffer from job burnout, and this can affect our teams. According to the Mayo Clinic, here's a list of questions to consider:[10]

- Do you question the value of your work?
- Do you drag yourself to work and have trouble getting started?
- Do you feel removed from your work and the people you work with?
- Have you lost patience with coworkers, customers, or clients?
- Do you lack the energy to do your job well?
- Is it hard to focus on your job?
- Do you feel little satisfaction from what you get done?

- Do you feel let down by your job?
- Do you doubt your skills and abilities?
- Are you using food, drugs, or alcohol to feel better or to numb how you feel?
- Have your sleep habits changed?
- Do you have headaches, stomach or bowel problems, or other physical complaints with no known cause?

If you answered yes to any of the above, you may be suffering from job burnout. Please consider speaking to a health care professional. For more information, please visit mayoclinic.org

How Can I Hold Myself Accountable as a Leader?

When we spoke about my former boss the Sheriff and bullying earlier, we talked about holding others as well as yourself accountable. If you allow a leader like Medusa to continue to stay on your team, causing hurt and harm to others, you also become part of the problem. As a leader, you must be willing to do your best to create a culture where everyone feels supported and can thrive. This also includes making the hard choices on who stays and who goes.

Too often, I listen to individuals use HR as the scapegoat. "It's HR's fault this happened; I went to them and complained. And they did nothing." So, I offer this analogy.

A few years ago, on a very cold New England winter day, the pipes in my mother's home froze and then burst. She was visiting me and not at home. We arrived back to discover a soaked house, most of it completely destroyed. The house was rebuilt over the next year, with the guidance of my mother, my brother, and my sister-in-law. Plumbers, contractors, and other individuals with expertise came in to assess and recommend how to rebuild and update the home.

We often take HR for granted. It is part of the plumbing, heating and cooling, electricity, and all the things behind the scenes that keep a home up and running, just like an organization. As employees, we may not know half the things happening, the technicalities or the details. But when the pipe bursts, or a toxic leader is found out, chaos ensues. And at the end of the day, it's up to the homeowner, or in our case the leader, to make the final decision on how to fix the mess and how to proceed. You can bring in advisors and expertise to help guide you, but the decision is yours. You are accountable for how the other leaders on your team behave and the toxic culture they are breeding.

Creating a culture where everyone is treated with respect shouldn't be a workplace luxury. It should be an essential requirement, basic working conditions, for our organizations. Individuals don't want another free meditation app, endless supply of fancy snacks, unlimited vacation days, free happy hours, and not another oversized hoodie, more mugs, and socks we will never wear. They want to be respected and valued. They want their contributions to be recognized and matter, and to work for leaders who support doing good work. Let's make sure bad bosses like Medusa exist only in the world of folklore and not actually in our hallways and on our Zoom screens.

Tips for Leaders to Stop Fear-Based Leadership

- Understand why you and others might be prone to leading with fear.
- Educate yourself on the negative impacts of fear-based leadership:
  - Fear kills communication.
  - Fear leads to decreased productivity.
  - Fear isolates team members.
  - Fear kills creativity and innovation.
  - Fear leads to burnout.
- Consider the following three questions when it comes to fear-based leadership:
  - Why are we suddenly labeling team members as detractors?
  - How do I spot the signs of burnout for my team? For myself?
  - How do I hold myself accountable and create a culture where everyone is respected?

7

The Boss Who
Punished Me
for Being Pregnant

I wanted to become a mother.

And I was scared to even think about family planning while working for Medusa. I remember a few colleagues who were able to become pregnant during that time, endured Medusa during their pregnancies, and then went out on leave. Some of them negotiated coming back to the organization after leave, but only if they returned to a different team. Some of them did not come back at all and got another job. I remember one colleague coming back from leave and handing in her resignation to Medusa her first week back. I watched the resignation conversation go down in that glass office. I secretly cheered.

After having a series of bad and then good and then bad bosses again, the timing never quite seemed right to have children. And what I learned is that often you have little to no control over the timing of when you are able to expand your family and what's happening in your career. My husband and I are now blessed to have two healthy, happy, and kind children. And while I wanted to have children, I was completely naive: I had no idea that Corporate America would view me differently once I became pregnant, and then became a mother. That a number of future bosses would think after becoming a mother, I was no longer capable of leading in the workplace.

Before I became pregnant with my daughter, I was up for a promotion. The vice president of the division said, "You are the clear front runner, you are on the list. I can definitely see you leading the team. The role will be listed shortly. Stay tuned for some interviews, we'll set them up."

I waited until 16 weeks to let the team know I was pregnant. As soon as I shared the news, the response from leadership was not a "Congratulations!" or "Wow, we are so happy for you!"

"You too? There must be something in the water here. Everyone is pregnant. I wonder how we are going to make it through business planning now."

And that was that.

The promotion opportunity mysteriously disappeared. The promotion I had been up for had been my boss's role. My boss moved on to another team, quickly forgetting about us. The role was never listed, there was no interview process. They hand-picked someone who was announced at a town hall meeting a week later.

Enter the Great Pretender. She had four children. She had been at the company for a while, was highly networked, and was very active in the women's employee resource group. She had even participated in a resource guide some of the women leaders had put together on "what to know about expecting here." She positioned herself as an advocate of moms in the workplace, both internally and all over her social media feed. Except when it came to me.

Because the moment she found out I was expecting, she punished me for being pregnant in subtle and not-so-subtle ways.

When she joined our team, I delicately asked her about my promotion path. Her response was

"Don't be in such a rush to get promoted. You have a growing family to think about now."

When I asked why I wasn't attending the leadership academy that month, her response was:

"You will be out on leave. You won't be able to action anything you learn until you come back." (I was still five months away from going out on leave.)

When I asked her why my projects were being moved to other team members, and why I was being removed from key meetings, her response was:

"We have to start transitioning projects and preparing for you to be out." (I was still four months away from going out on leave.)

When I asked her why I wasn't presenting at the annual customer meeting, her response was:

"Oh, you are close to having that baby. You stay back and rest." (I was still three months away from going out on leave.)

When I asked her to review my performance goals and career interests before going out on leave, her response was:

"Once you hold that baby in your arms, everything changes. You may not even want to come back!"

It was because of the Great Pretender that I was educated on the pregnancy penalty. I was sidelined, penalized, disregarded, and slowly being pushed out because I was pregnant. She did it with a smile, a wink, with concern for myself and my family, with a genuine feeling, pretense, that she knew what was best for me, and with complete conviction and little room for me to make my own decisions on what was best for my career.

She hired a consultant, who was her friend, to backfill me for the six months I was out on leave. I transitioned the work I had left, had final check-ins with my team members on their performance to date, and put on my out-of-office message. I was officially out on leave for the next six months ready to welcome our daughter to our family.

Except I wasn't.

Three weeks after my daughter was born, the first text came from the Great Pretender:

> "Hope you and baby are great! Can you please log in quick and send me that file? I can't seem to find it anywhere."

Of course I responded. I rushed to accommodate her, make her happy, show her I was a team player. It was a small request and only took me a few minutes. And with that small request, the flood gates opened.

> "How are you feeling? Do you have that email summarizing why our innovation is being discontinued in those grocery channels?"
>
> "Hope you are doing well today. Can you please forward those slides you worked on for the last quarterly update?"
>
> "Do you remember how much we agreed to pay the agency for that campaign? Send a pic of that cutie!"

"Could you log in and release your team's performance reviews? You are the only person who has access to do this."

"Can you talk to the consultant today? Maybe when the baby is napping? She needs a debrief from you on each team member for next week's company talent review."

While the Great Pretender was quick to dismiss me when I was pregnant, she aggressively reached out to me over and over again while I was out on leave. And I made the mistake of engaging with her and doing work. Wanting to make a good impression, wanting that promotion when I came back, and wanting to show her my value, that I could be a mother and still lead at work.

When I returned to work, I was greeted by many colleagues who were excited and some who were surprised to see me:

- "How was your vacation?"
- "You came back? Already? You sure you don't want to go part-time?"
- "I am jealous of all those pumping 'breaks' you get to take."
- "If you are here, who is watching and raising that precious baby?"
- "Are you planning on having more kids?"

My husband, for the record, received none of the above commentary when he returned to work after just two weeks of leave.

On that very first day, I received an email from the Great Pretender, cc'ing human resources (HR), saying that I had to immediately put a team member on a performance improvement plan. And this individual had not been a fit on the team for months. When I asked why they didn't give this team member the feedback sooner, she laughed and said, "Well, I was waiting for you to come back and handle it."

The next week, I had my annual performance review with the Great Pretender. She gave me a 2 rating. This was on a scale of 1–5, a forced company bell curve, with 5 being the highest rating. And the only time I had ever heard of anyone getting the 1 rating was if they were being terminated. Most women on leave I knew got a 3 rating, which was meeting expectations.

When I asked why I was getting such a low rating she responded, "Well, the business fell off a cliff this year."

"I didn't work for six months of the year, so I am not clear how I am being held responsible," I responded. Completely puzzled by the performance review.

"Listen, you can make me out to be the wicked stepmother here, but the rating is the rating," she growled at me. I nodded my head, clenched my teeth, and swallowed that 2 rating and a bonus, which after taxes, was so small that it couldn't even help subsidize my Starbucks obsession.

Maybe I should have changed her nickname to the Wicked Stepmother instead.

The following week, the Great Pretender handed me an invoice to pay out of my team budget. I was to pay her friend who was the consultant, who had covered my role while I was on leave. I looked at the invoice. I couldn't stop staring at the amount owed.

This consultant made twice as much as I did in the six months she covered my role.

(My team later told me that much of the time when this consultant was on conference calls, you would hear her vacuuming, cooking loudly, and answering the doorbell ringing in the background. She often forgot to put herself on mute.)

Almost a year later, after a new vice president arrived, I left the team and transferred divisions. My career conversations with the Great Pretender circled around the same topic: her questioning my ambition and my desire to get promoted. As other women joined her team, and became pregnant, they reached out to me to share similar stories of the Great Pretender. They just couldn't wrap their head around a mother in the workplace pretending to champion other mothers, being on panels for International Women's Day, recording recruiting videos for the company's website, and more. Yet in reality, it was all a pretense. A fellow mother helping to perpetuate the pregnancy penalty and the motherhood penalty in our workplaces.

★★★★★★

The bias pregnant women and mothers face in the workplace is real.

Our workplaces weren't built with pregnant women in mind. According to the Pew Research Center, in the early 1960s, only 44% of women worked during their pregnancy.[1] Historically many companies not just expected, but required women to quit when they became pregnant.[2] Fast-forward to today:

- 70% of pregnant women work during their pregnancy.[3]
- One in five pregnant women are scared to tell their boss their pregnancy news.[4]
- One in five mothers says they have experienced pregnancy discrimination at work.[5]
- According to a *New York Times* investigation, some of the nation's largest companies "systematically deny advancement to pregnant workers and fire those who complain."[6]
- The Equal Employment Opportunity Commission has seen "the number of pregnancy discrimination claims filed annually steadily rising for two decades and hovering near an all-time high."[7]

And once women become mothers, they face a whole new set of challenges. According to research from the Harvard Kennedy School:[8]

- Competency ratings:
  - 10% lower for mothers versus women without children among otherwise equal candidates.
- Commitment to job:
  - Mothers were considered to be 12.1% points less committed to their jobs versus women without children.
  - Fathers were perceived as being 5% points more committed versus men without children.
  - Mothers were rated 6.4% points lower with regard to commitment versus men without children.
- Recommended for hire:
  - Mothers were 6 times less likely than women without children and 3.35 times less likely than men without children to be recommended for hire.
- Promotion opportunities:
  - Women without children are 8.2 times more likely to be recommended for a promotion than mothers.

There are many more statistics. And behind every statistic is a story. A story of a bad boss like the Great Pretender, who had the power to dismiss, minimize, or slowly push pregnant women and mothers out of their teams and even out of their organizations. And a bad boss who had the power to slow down, sideline, or completely derail their careers.

Understanding the Pregnancy and Motherhood Penalty, and the Fatherhood Premium

Understanding the following terms, and stopping them from playing out in our workplaces, can prevent us and others from becoming that bad boss.

Pregnancy Penalty

For many women, the pregnancy penalty often starts before the motherhood penalty kicks in. It's the bias and the inflexibility, the sidelining, penalizing, and dismissing of women in the workplace who become pregnant. According to the Harvard Kennedy School, research shows that "visibly pregnant women are judged as being less committed to their jobs, less dependable, less authoritative, more emotional, and more irrational" than otherwise equal women who are not pregnant.[9] This bias can snowball into lasting economic disadvantages that can have a devastating impact on a woman's career and her family.

Motherhood Penalty

The motherhood penalty is the price women in the workplace pay for becoming mothers and expanding their families. Mothers in our workplaces are less likely to be hired for new roles and offered promotions, while earning lower salaries.[10] They will be held to a higher standard than fathers and than women without children. According to the World Economic Forum, the motherhood penalty makes up 80% of the gender pay gap.[11]

Fatherhood Premium

The fatherhood premium, also known as the fatherhood bonus, occurs because of the belief that fathers are committed to their careers, they are more stable, and they are more deserving. Mothers can often be stereotyped as being exhausted, distracted, less committed to their careers, and just a disheveled mess.

(continued)

(*continued*)

According to the National Women's Law Center, mothers working full-time and year-round earn 71 cents to every dollar paid to fathers working full time, year-round.[12] This gap in earnings robs mothers of $1,667 every month or $20,000 every year. This gap is worse for mothers of color. Latina and Native American mothers working full-time, year-round earn 51 cents to every dollar paid to white fathers. For Latina and Native American mothers, this can add up to losses of $39,000 a year. Black mothers working full-time, year-round, earn 52 cents for every dollar paid to white fathers. For Black mothers, this can add up to losses of $38,000 a year.

Research also shows that mothers were recommended a "7.9% lower starting salary than women without children, which is 8.6% lower than the recommended starting salary for fathers."[13] The trend was reversed among men: fathers were offered a significantly higher starting salary than men without children.[14]

Here's how we can advocate for pregnant women and mothers in our workplaces and avoid being the bad boss like the Great Pretender who punishes them.

Interrupt Your Own Bias Toward Pregnant Women and Mothers in the Workplace

As I discovered in my career, even mothers can have a bias toward other mothers in the workplace, whether they are aware of it or not. Just because we identify as being from the same community, or having a similar lived experience, doesn't make us immune to having bias.

And as someone who is on a mission to create fair and equitable workplaces for all, with much self-reflection, I realized I had also internalized societal expectations of women and mothers.

I am the proud daughter of Indian immigrant parents; my younger brother and I were born and raised in the United States. My father was a mechanical engineer and the primary earner, my mother was the lead parent and worked inside the home. When I was in high school, my mother entered the workforce to become a teacher. Growing up, I can't recall any Aunty in my community working outside the home, and they all were mothers. (We never called adults by their first name, we always used Aunty or Uncle as a sign of respect. We have passed this tradition on to our children as well.)

My parents had the same expectations of my brother and me: we would both make education our number-one priority, pursuing undergraduate and graduate degrees, and join the workforce. And yet, I am certain the community I grew up in, the influence of media, and the greater world tried to condition me to think a woman's primary role is to be a caregiver. I continue to struggle with guilt and shame of what it means to be a good mother and what it means to have a successful career and be a good leader. We each have to self-reflect and do the internal work to ask ourselves if our attitudes toward mothers have evolved, and if not, why.

Consider the following questions:

- When a woman tells you she's going to become a mother, do you question if she will return to work after her leave?
- When a man tells you he's going to become a father, do you question if he will return to work after leave?
- Do you try to be helpful if she's pregnant? Do you tell her to work from home, remove her from certain meetings, and take projects off her plate when she hasn't asked for any accommodations?

- When a woman becomes a mother, do you think that she will want to go part-time and want more flexibility? How about fathers?
- Do you think that a mother on your team is less ambitious? That she may be less interested in challenging assignments and not interested in promotion opportunities?
- Do you think that a father on your team is less ambitious? That he may be less interested in challenging assignments and not interested in promotion opportunities?
- Do you pause when hiring or promoting women of a certain age range because you believe they will just become pregnant and leave the team?

Self-reflecting on our own attitudes, beliefs, and biases is a key step in preventing ourselves from slipping into bad boss territory and holding mothers back in the workplace.

Ask Pregnant Women and Mothers How You Can Help Support Them

When a woman shares her pregnancy news with you, or news of expanding her family, start by congratulating her. Then ask this simple question: How can I support you during this time?

She may not have that answer in that moment; let her know that you are open to follow-up conversations. By leading with this question, we stop ourselves from making any assumptions about pregnant women and mothers on what they do or don't need.

Here are additional things to share with her in follow-up conversations:

- "Please know I am here to help support whatever workplace accommodations you may need during your pregnancy."

- "I am happy to review the leave policy with you and connect you with HR if you have further questions or need support."
- "If you would like to connect with other pregnant women, mothers, and parents here, I'm happy to make introductions."
- "I'll be taking the lead on a transition plan for when you are out; closer to your leave date. I would love your input on it."
- "Let's set up time to discuss your annual performance goals and career goals before you go out."

Let's not fall into the trap of drawing comparisons from our own lived experiences, or what we have seen other women do or not do, when trying to be a supportive leader. By continuing to have an open dialogue, we ensure that we aren't making any decisions about her career for her. It's up to her to decide what she wants in a career.

Interrupt Bias to Educate Team Members

It's all of our jobs to interrupt bias to educate our team members who may be questioning or doubting the value of mothers in our workplaces. In fact, according to a Bright Horizons study, "41% of employed Americans perceive working moms to be less devoted to their work."[15] When we see something, we must say something to ensure we don't miss out on the talent and potential of pregnant women and mothers in our organizations.

I coach leaders to use open-ended questions to get us all to self-reflect on bias, help evolve our views, and have more productive conversations. Here are some questions to ask (adjusting as needed depending on the scenario):

- Did Mita indicate to us she is not coming back from leave? Why wouldn't we include her on the slate of candidates for this promotion?

- I noticed Mita is getting a low performance rating when she was out for six months of the year on leave. Can someone please remind me of the policy we have for how we ensure we fairly rate individuals on leave?
- Have we asked Mita what her career goals are? Has she told us she wants to be working part-time now?
- I noticed Mita is no longer leading this project and she's not scheduled to go on leave for another five months. Can you help me understand why she's no longer leading?
- Hank also became a father recently. Are we concerned that he's no longer committed to his job in the same way we are speaking about Mita, who is also a new parent?

When we don't challenge the bias and the assumption that women will be or are the primary caretakers of their families, we can deny them promotions, raises, and opportunities to grow and advance their careers. Bad bosses perpetuate the stigma of pregnancy and motherhood in our workplaces. Their behavior, and the decisions they make, can sideline or derail a woman's career. And every time a bad boss punishes a pregnant woman or a mother in the workplace, they are ultimately helping to widen the gender pay gap.

However, good leaders remind everyone that pregnant women and mothers are not any less capable or less committed to their work. They recognize and celebrate their talents, and remind everyone, even the bad bosses like the Great Pretender, that pregnant women and mothers are some of the most exceptional employees and leaders.

**Tips for Leaders to Create Team Cultures
Inclusive of Pregnant Women and Mothers**

Educate yourself on the statistics to understand the bias pregnant women and mothers face in the workplace; listen to and learn from their stories.

- Understand and watch out for how the pregnancy and motherhood penalty, and fatherhood premium, play out in our workplaces.
- Advocate for pregnant women and mothers in our workplaces:
  - Interrupt your own bias toward pregnant women and mothers in the workplace.
    - Self-reflect on your expectations of mothers in the workplace and push to evolve your own thinking.
  - Ask pregnant women and mothers how you can help support them:
    - Never assume what they want or need in their careers.
  - Interrupt bias to educate team members:
    - Use open-ended questions to challenge bias and have productive conversations.
- Remember that it's against the law to discriminate against individuals based on pregnancy, childbirth, or related medical conditions.[16] Consult your legal team for more support and learn more at the US Equal Employment Opportunity Commission[17] and at and The National Women's Law Center.[18]
- Finally, if you are looking for more specific guidance on how to create an inclusive culture for all parents, particularly when it comes to leadership behavior and company policies, please check out my first book, *Reimagine Inclusion: Debunking 13 Myths to Transform Your Workplace.*

8

The Boss Who Was Incredibly Kind and Completely Incompetent at His Job

Up until this point in my career, I had dealt with a wide range of bad bosses who weren't just bad at being bosses but were also mean. Some were unkind, some full of anger, and some were bitter. Some were rude and some inconsiderate. Some of them thrived on lashing out at their teams, who were in survival mode. Some showed little to no emotion because they were so disengaged.

So, I had never worked for a bad boss who was just incredibly kind.

Enter the Grinner.

He always had a big grin on his face. Nothing could seem to put him in a bad mood.

He never missed a team member's birthday, showing up with or sending to their home their favorite cupcakes or sweet treats.

He always asked us how we were doing in our one-on-one meetings and genuinely wanted to know about our family, friends, pets, and hobbies outside of work. He knew the names of our kids and their ages, too.

He never called us on vacation, sent late-night texts or emails, or expected us to work on the weekends.

He always had a joke for us that his teenage boys had shared, striving to be the cool dad.

And he was completely incompetent.

And when I mean incompetent, I mean this: The Grinner didn't know how to lead his weekly team meetings. So, he had each of us rotate responsibilities to run the meeting, coming up with agenda topics, and all the while he grinned. He rarely offered any items for us to discuss. He would be incredibly supportive, peppering our time together with "Well done" and "That's amazing" and "I am so proud of this team." He never hired a chief of staff, even though he hired for a number of other less critical roles. So we all had to pitch in and do our part to keep the team running smoothly.

The Grinner didn't know or understand how to do basic calculations. When the president of the division sent him a text asking him what the sell-through rate was for our latest innovation at a key customer, he panicked. He forwarded me the text and said, "What does this mean? What do I say?" I emailed him the formula for the simple calculation and also sent him the weekly spreadsheet from sales that included the metric. I doubt he had ever opened that document.

"You are a rock star!" He responded.

The Grinner didn't know how to build decks. He had us build every single slide for every single deck. He never made any changes, he never had any comments, he never took credit for any of the work. He would respond in person or over email saying, "How lucky am I to work with all of you" and "You guys knocked this out of the park" and "This is outstanding work!"

The Grinner didn't know how or what to present. So every presentation to leadership, he would kick it off with having memorized a handful of key stats and key talking points, some of which weren't important and some of which weren't relevant for the discussion at hand. And then he would shower the team with praise and hand it over to us to present.

The Grinner also didn't know how to give meaningful feedback. Other than his sunshine-filled phrases of "Keep up the great work" and "You are killing it" and "Keep doing what you are doing," he had nothing of real substance to say. He didn't really understand what we did so he couldn't comment on it. During performance review time, two of my colleagues and I compared our written performance evaluations. It was the same copy, same language, except for our names. We all had different jobs and had received not *essentially* the same review, but rather the same exact performance review.

And as incompetent as the Grinner was . . . he was just so damn likable. So, for some of the team, it was hard to stay angry at him.

He was genuine. He listened to understand and not to just respond. He asked questions and really wanted to know the answers (even if he didn't know what to do with those answers). He always greeted everyone by their name (used the right names for the right person, perfected the pronunciation, and asked if he was saying your name right). He didn't seek attention, he didn't take credit for our work (he understood that if we were shining, that shine would rub off on him somehow and make him look good).

He used humor appropriately (mostly bad parenting jokes). He praised us often. He never passed judgment. He put his phone away and paid attention (not sure what he actually absorbed when others were speaking).

He left a strong first impression. He had those wrinkle-free Brooks Brothers collared shirts with sometimes dark jeans and other times khaki pants. He smelled of the men's signature cologne that we made (not doused in it like Medusa and her Chanel No. 5). He could easily have been cast as a contestant on *The Bachelorette*, or even hold his own and be the bachelor and headline the show.

And yes, he was always smiling wide. Grinning ear to ear.

"If he was a woman, he would have been gone a long time ago," lamented my colleague Julia, sipping her glass of chardonnay. "Do you think they would have kept around an incompetent but likable woman for this long?"

"Can women leaders even be likable?"

"Well, if he were a woman, he never would have gotten the job," someone else chimed in.

"Oh, I have worked for incompetent women leaders," added someone else. "There are so many incompetent leaders who fail up."

"Except women don't have the luxury of failing up the way men do."

Our team happy hour outings circled around the same questions over and over again, as we sipped on our drinks, munched on mozzarella cheese sticks and chicken nachos, and presented new theories on the situation at hand:

How could someone as incompetent as the Grinner still be employed?

How could management not see how incompetent he was and do something?

Did everyone just really like him that much that it didn't matter that he couldn't do his job?

What did we think was on his performance evaluation?
What feedback did his boss give him?
Who was protecting him and why?

I knew that the Grinner was a bad boss. And because I had
dealt with so many other horrible bosses before him, on some
days he just didn't seem as bad. It could be worse, right? Until
one Friday late afternoon, he dropped a last-minute assignment
from leadership that needed to be completed, due first thing
Monday morning. I was livid. I had reached my tipping point
when it came to the Grinner. Suddenly, I couldn't handle the
incompetence anymore.

"This will take the team all weekend to complete," I snapped,
completely exasperated. "Our weekend is completely blown up.
And I have three kids' birthday parties this weekend and soccer
practice and swim lessons . . ."

"I am sorry," he offered. "What can I do to help?"

"Nothing, you can't do anything to help," I snapped at him,
completed agitated. "I'll see you on Monday."

That night, my husband walked into the kitchen juggling
two cheese pizzas from a local shop and two pints of ice cream,
a box of rainbow sprinkles, and a pack of cones.

"From your boss," he said, gesturing at the items. "He sent a
card with the delivery."

*Thank you for your hard work. I hope your kids enjoy the dinner
and sweet treats! Please call me if I can help at all this weekend.*

I bit into a slice of gooey cheese pizza as I revised some
slides. I checked my email to find an Uber Eats gift card he had
sent me for a Saturday meal with the kids. I sighed.

The Grinner wasn't smart enough to do his job. But he was
smart enough to know that he needed me and the other team
members to do his job. That part he had figured out.

About 18 months later, the Grinner was promoted. He moved abroad to lead a business unit to get global experience. The organization only sent leaders on assignments outside the United States when they really wanted to invest in them. So he continued to fail up.

After that, I lost track of the Grinner. I heard from others that he kept failing up. And up.

Years went by until one day I received a random message from him on LinkedIn. I couldn't believe he had reached out, and I wondered what he had to say to me.

His message read: "You are a rock star! Keep up the great work!"

★★★★★

According to one study, 24% of employees are currently working for the worst boss they have ever had in their career.[1] And what behaviors have earned these individuals the worst boss label? The leading bad behavior is this: bosses who don't know what they are doing. 46% of employees said these bad bosses were "incompetent."[2] And according to Society of Human Resource Management, similar to my former boss, the Grinner, 36% of employees say their boss doesn't know how to lead a team.[3]

Another study from the Tippie College of Business uncovers the factor age plays in how we deal with incompetent bad bosses:[4]

- Employees are "willing to accept an incompetent boss who is older and more experienced than they are."
- They are less likely to accept "incompetence if the boss is younger and less experienced."
- If they think their boss, who is younger than they and has fewer years of experience, is incompetent, they question the fairness of promotions at their company. This can affect team morale and ultimately productivity.

- They are "more likely to accept an incompetent older boss by convincing themselves that the employer's promotion system is fair, so the boss may not be as bad as they think."

Years later, I realized that when I was working for the Grinner, I justified the unfairness in the system to myself. Because he was older and had more experience than I, although not by much. And as a team, we did spend the time covering for him, doing his work, and propping him up like a puppet, as one colleague had once described. Given the power dynamics at play in our workplaces, I am not sure we had any choice but to prop up the incredibly kind and completely incompetent bad boss. Unless we no longer wanted to work there. And according to a Gallup study, 50% of employees quit to escape that incompetent, bad boss.[5] I said goodbye to a handful of peers who could no longer tolerate the Grinner. I and a handful of others were the last ones standing.

So why do we let kind and incompetent bosses stay in our workplaces? Here are some ways I have heard leaders rationalize the decision to let them stay:

- He's the kind of leader we need right now to turn morale around. He will learn all that business stuff.
- She's a lifer. She's not going anywhere, and she would be too expensive to fire.
- Isn't it the team's job to get the work done anyway?
- That guy went to college with the CEO's brother. We all know he's clueless, and the CEO wants people around her whom she can trust.
- All I hear about is more kindness in the workplace, *blah, blah, blah*. He is the nicest person I know here. So what exactly is the team's problem?
- Would you rather have a boss who was a jerk and didn't know what she was doing?

Unlike the mean, angry, or even cruel incompetent boss, the kind and incompetent boss can be easier for many of us to justify and rationalize away their bad boss behavior. But *they are so kind, they didn't mean it, they will get better, give them another shot, and listen, everyone likes them, they get along with the team.* Shouldn't that count for something?

I would argue that kind and incompetent bad bosses can be even more costly to a company than the mean and incompetent bad bosses. The kindness may mask the real issue at hand: that this individual is not capable of doing their job and leading. Because they are "kind," it washes away their incompetency and excuses their inability to do their job. And this incompetency chips away at team members with a cost to their own personal health and a cost to the company: unplanned absences costs companies approximately $431 billion per year.[6] And employees calling in sick because they don't want to be at work costs companies up to $86 billion per year.[7] Because as my colleague once said, "Sometimes we have no more energy to prop up that bad boss no matter how many smiles they flash our way and no matter how many boxes of pizza they send to our homes."

Are You Fit to Lead?

During the course of my career, I have been in roles where I didn't know what I was doing. I have enough awareness to know I needed help, but my ego might get in the way. Because as leaders, we don't want to show our weakness or be vulnerable. We are the boss, we are supposed to be in charge, we are supposed to know what to do. Bosses don't often admit that they need help. And that's one of the differences between bad bosses and good leaders: good leaders regularly ask for and seek out support to make themselves better leaders and individuals.

Consider the following questions to self-reflect on:

- Have I been onboarded properly into this role? Have I done an audit to understand what the gaps are and what I need to learn and understand? If my boss hasn't or won't create an onboarding plan for me, can I do this myself with the assistance of my team and peers?
- Have I asked my team what they think my areas of opportunity are? Have I asked for their support in focusing on these areas?
- Have I asked my boss to support me taking specific courses to upskill myself on competencies and expertise I am lacking? If they won't provide support, have I taken the time to research some of these areas online on my own?
- Have I considered finding mentors in the organization who would sit with me for 30 minutes each week, helping me upskill on a particular topic?
- Do I really want to be managing and leading this team? Am I better off as an individual contributor? Have I asked anyone in the organization for advice on this?

Finally, there's a difference between not having the competency to do the job or the ability or interest to learn on the job, versus suffering from imposter syndrome. As my friend and coach Christy DeSantis says, "We go through moments of imposter syndrome (when we believe we just got lucky to be where we are or that someone will find out that we don't really know what we're doing). Or we don't feel comfortable acknowledging what we've achieved because we fear we might appear arrogant if we do so. For women, this can be especially challenging if they have ever been told during a performance review that they are too aggressive or they speak too much in meetings."[8]

Let's make sure we are setting ourselves and other leaders up for success. Let's stop enabling and helping individuals to fail up.

Who Do We Think Looks Like a Leader?

According to a *USA TODAY* analysis of the named executive officers at S&P 100 companies, white men still run Corporate America:[9]

- Of the 533 named executive officers across these corporations, white men represent 7 in 10.
- Women, just 90 of them, make up 17% of named officers. Only 17 women of color are named executive officers.
- Of those companies, about one in seven had executive teams that were made up of only white men.

Additionally, "White men today are even more likely than their grandfathers to be managers despite a diversifying workforce and evidence from research studies that diverse companies outperform peers that are not," says Alexandra Kalev, an associate professor of sociology and anthropology at Tel Aviv University.[10]

Research from *Social Science Quarterly* shows that for men, being attractive played a significant role in their professional success.[11] They moved up the corporate ladder the fastest, including promotions and access to more competitive jobs and were making the most. Other research shows that "many of the characteristics people use to describe strong, capable leaders are masculine."[12]

Academic researcher Alexi Gugushvili found that women's attractiveness is often characterized by "weak" feminine traits, like being agreeable and passive. He pointed out that, "while men are expected to lead with decisiveness, women are discouraged from taking up jobs with a high level of authority and given harmful labels such as difficult or bossy, because it's seen as unattractive."[13]

Unlike the Grinner, women can suffer from the "likability trap" in our workplaces. We can be liked enough to be given a seat at the table, given that promotion, and given an opportunity to lead. But if we are too likable, then others may think we are a pushover, weak, too kind, and just not qualified to lead no matter how many receipts we have, no matter how many points we have on the board. No matter how competent we are.

If we have been conditioned to believe that leaders should look and act a certain way, we might be more willing to give them a pass or give them more chances to succeed. We have to fight our biases: understanding the difference between the confidence someone exudes and how attractive we think they are, versus their competence and capabilities.

Are We Setting Our Leaders Up for Success?

As we examine our definitions of who a leader can be, we must ensure we are doing our best to set them up for success. A poor onboarding experience, whether the leader is an external or internal hire/move, can lead to high turnover rates, decreased productivity, and increased costs for the team. Employees who have a poor onboarding experience are much more likely to be disengaged at work. According to Gallup, disengaged employees cost the business money: "approximately 18% of their salary."[14] And what if the boss is the one who hasn't been onboarded or upskilled properly? What impact can that have on the team?

Ask yourself the following:

- When a new leader joins from an external company, do you just ask the assistant to set up 25 one-on-one meetings for them and dump a bunch of other meetings on their calendar? Or do you take the time to craft a thoughtful 30-day onboarding plan?

- Do you have a three-month and six-month check-in to see how they are acclimating?
- Do you ask their team members at least once a year how their leader is performing, allowing anonymous feedback? Do you dismiss the feedback or try to process and understand things that may surprise you?
- When you are doing performance reviews, are you specific on their areas of opportunity or providing vague or generic feedback that can be applied to anyone on the team?

If we don't set our leaders up for success, don't onboard them properly, don't support them, or promote them too quickly, let's not be surprised when they start exhibiting bad boss behavior.

Are They Fit to Do the Job?

Finally, we need to stop to consider if this individual is actually fit to do the job. Are they capable of sharing their expertise and leading the team? Or are we convincing ourselves that they will just figure it out along the way?

I watched too many leaders continue to advance someone's career based off their potential and not performance. They will take a bet on them, move them up because they just like them, advocate for them because they are friends. Or because something about this person seems familiar: the individual reminds them of themselves.

Too many of our workplaces are set up to recognize high performers, outstanding individual contributors through promotions. And that promotion usually means you are now responsible for other people's careers. Yale Professor Kelly Shue and her colleagues' study shows that organizations still prioritize employees' performance as an individual contributor versus their potential to lead people when deciding whom to promote.[15] This is similar behavior to how factories operated in the 1960s, when workers were promoted into leadership roles based on manufacturing efficiency and not based on if they could actually lead teams.[16]

So stop just promoting people to the next level. Help them thrive in their career so their teams can thrive. Give them the tools and training and support they need if you do decide to promote them. Or consider an individual contributor track for them where they can continue to advance and grow, get paid more, without ever having to manage another individual.

We can mistake a company full of incredibly likable Grinners, who just happen to look like they came from central casting, as a sign of a healthy culture. And if the team is spending most of their energy and time propping these bad bosses up like puppets, they will one by one by one make plans to escape this theater that they find themselves trapped in. After all, they didn't sign up to be a puppeteer. That wasn't part of the job description.

Tips on Ensuring Bosses are Ready to Lead Teams

- Understand what it costs the company and your teams when you protect and keep incredibly nice and completely incompetent bosses.
- Ask yourself the question, "Are you fit to lead?" and identify what your areas of opportunity might be. Work to upskill yourself to become a better leader and avoid becoming a bad boss.
- Consider the following questions to ensure you aren't enabling or helping bad bosses to continue to fail up:
  - Who do we think looks like a leader?
    - Fight our biases: understand the difference between the confidence someone exudes and how attractive we think they are, versus their competence and capabilities.
  - Are we setting our leaders up for success?
    - Onboard them, train them, and support them. Regularly check in with them and also with their teams on how the leader is doing. Don't ignore what you hear.
  - Are they fit to do the job?
    - Stop rewarding strong individual contributors with a promotion that involves leading people. Don't promote just off of their individual performance; promote based on their ability to lead others and be responsible for their careers.

9

The Boss Who Was Filled with Toxic Positivity

While the Grinner was always smiling, he was very measured and steady when it came to his emotions. He didn't get overly happy or overly sad. Perhaps because he was incredibly incompetent, nothing at work seemed to truly phase him. It was hard to get a strong emotional reaction out of him.

When it came to bad bosses who exhibited extreme emotion, I had mostly experienced a range of anger, including full-on temper tantrums, throwing items at me and others in a fit of rage, and random outbursts of shouting in the workplace. I hadn't ever worked for a boss who was oozing with sunshine, spoke to you as if they were reciting inspirational Instagram quotes, and walked around snapping, clapping, and randomly high-fiving those who passed by their desks.

How could someone like that even be a bad boss?

Enter the Cheerleader.

He was one of the company's division presidents. He had been promoted through the ranks quickly, and unlike the Grinner, he wasn't failing up. He had a photographic memory and could spit out stats about your business that you had long forgotten. He had a strong pulse on what our customers needed and was an incredible negotiator. He pulled his own data, built his own slides, and wrote his own talk track. He was a masterful storyteller and knew how to capture the attention of an audience. He was incredibly well respected in the organization, always dressed in a full dark suit and tie. And he knew how to sell a magical vision that we would all buy into. And he was like the corporate Pied Piper: we would follow him all around the office.

Like any good cheerleader, he used his strength, his endurance, and his skills to be an excellent spirit raiser. An entertainer. Rallying the troops, getting the crowd going. Clapping, smiling, snapping, cheering, and sometimes, yes, even a spin.

I had never witnessed anything like this in my career. A boss who garnered so much positive energy, so much excitement, so much enthusiasm. We all wanted to be in his presence. We wanted to be in meetings with him. We wanted to meet with him one-on-one. We would stay late, take weekend calls, do whatever we needed, to get the job done. I once stayed up until 3:30 a.m. to work on a deck for him for a meeting where he was presenting at 8 a.m. the next morning. I remember this night vividly because my son was sick and getting up every two hours wailing. I was then up at 6 a.m. to make sure my boss had everything he needed for the meeting.

We would go above and beyond for him, even when he didn't ask us to.

And slowly, I realized, all the sunshine, rainbows, and lollipops started to fade. Those fist pumps in the air started to get tiresome. This feeling that we were part of a mission, bigger and greater than ourselves, that we were in fact saving the world, felt phony. Because the truth was this: We weren't saving any lives. We weren't 911 dispatchers, emergency room nurses, firefighters, ambulance drivers, or crisis counselors. We were just selling cereal. And lots and lots of it.

The Cheerleader had created a culture of toxic positivity.

The Cheerleader surrounded himself with yes people. He wouldn't take no for an answer. His chief of staff, his executive assistant, and a senior manager (the trifecta as we called them) would always agree with him, intervene when we challenged him, and would inevitably respond, "Yes, yes, we can make this happen!" They shielded him from the reality, because they knew "no" wasn't an option for him. They led the charge to get us all to overpromise and overcommit. Which inevitably led to underdelivering, disappointment, and complete frustration.

The Cheerleader was constantly showering us with praise. And it was always completely over the top. So you actually never knew when he was being sincere or genuine, or flattering you to get something out of you. When I took on a new assignment under the Cheerleader, I had seven people on my team. One resigned my first week on the job, and in the days and weeks to follow, five people were rotated or promoted off my team. It was just me and one other team member, as the company announced a hiring freeze for the rest of the year. In a portfolio that was in double-digit decline. All of a sudden, it seemed like people didn't want to eat cereal for breakfast, lunch, and dinner. And I couldn't blame them.

"You are the only one who can do this for the company, this is why I let all these people move on from the team," he reassured me, patting me on the back. "You can backfill them next year, I promise. I believe in you."

I was only able to hire one individual, almost another seven months later.

The Cheerleader always wanted us to be happy. We always had to be smiling big like a Cheshire Cat, like we were streaming live and needed to be on and stay positive and be joyful for hundreds of people potentially watching us. To see how happy we all were. He would ask us why we weren't smiling, tell us to smile big, and remind us that a simple smile could change our workday. He would use his fingers and pull a smile on his face when he walked by and didn't see me and others smiling. On some days, I wasn't unhappy. This was just my resting face expression. And that wasn't cheerful enough for the Cheerleader.

"Don't worry, be happy" was one of the bumper stickers on his car.

"A smile is a curve that sets everything straight," was a sticker on his laptop.

"The world always looks brighter from behind a smile," was printed on a yellow t-shirt he once wore under his suit jacket when presenting to our incoming class of interns.

And one day, during a team meeting, the Cheerleader had one of his most "toxic positive" ideas ever.

"Let's add another million dollars to the forecast this year," he shouted with excitement.

"We can do this! I believe in you! Let's get it done!" He shouted, clapping his hands and standing up in our team meeting. He was rallying the troops again, walking around the conference room. He alternated between patting team members on the back and offering his signature fist pumps.

My colleague and I looked at each other in disbelief. Our head of supply chain had just alerted us that our latest cereal product was selling faster than what we could produce and offer to customers. And one of our facilities could no longer produce this particular product. The Cheerleader knew all of this, and yet forced us to add an additional million dollars to the forecast. We tried to protest, show him the data, pull up the emails, bring in the head of supply chain. It didn't matter. We were adding the million dollars to the forecast. *No* was not an option.

No amount of wishful thinking, positive vibes, or a can-do attitude could get us to meet this new forecast target.

During my annual year-end performance, I was informed that I wouldn't be getting a merit increase that year. My bonus also would be substantially less than the prior year. When I asked why, the Cheerleader smiled and said, "We missed the forecast by a million dollars, and so I couldn't justify giving you a merit increase and a hefty bonus," he exclaimed. "And you are one of my all-stars, you are an amazing leader. I know the more teams you lead, the more people you lead, you are just going to soar higher and higher!"

About 18 months later, the Cheerleader moved on to lead another division. My cheekbones and facial muscles thanked me for no longer working for the Cheerleader. I no longer had to smile on demand or have "my smile screensaver" on all day long at work. I could freely and happily work with my resting face.

With most of my bad bosses, I have learned many lessons from them. And I also haven't kept in touch with any of them. Last I heard from a friend, the Cheerleader is still soaring high in Corporate America. He's apparently working on getting his keynote speech ready for an intriguing TEDx Talk: leading with optimism to get the best out of your teams.

★★★★★

Being happy and positive at work can be a win-win for employees and organizations.[1] According to University of Oxford research, an extensive study showed that employees are 13% more productive when happy.[2] According to Shawn Achor, the author of *The Happiness Advantage*, positivity in the work-place, grounded in gratitude and appreciation, can lead to three times more creativity, 23% fewer fatigue symptoms, and 37%

greater sales.[3] And finally Better Up, one of the largest mental health and coaching startups,[4] offers that having a positive mindset can lead individuals to better problem-solve, have a greater ability to adapt to change, and have stronger leadership skills.[5] But what happens when your boss decides to weaponize positivity in the workplace?

Over the course of my career, I have seen bad bosses time and time again practice toxic positivity. No matter how bad or stressful the situation is, or how difficult the circumstances, these bad bosses believe that being optimistic, positive, or thinking positively will change the outcome. They convince themselves of this and spread this toxic positivity to their teams. They deny, minimize, and invalidate what their teams are experiencing. By practicing toxic positivity, they put the responsibility on individuals to try to survive and persevere in broken and dysfunctional environments, without addressing the root causes at hand.

Are You Optimistic or Full of Toxic Positivity?

My Indian immigrant parents gave me many gifts, including an incredible work ethic. From a young age, I believed hard work could solve any problem. If you just worked hard enough, if you just put in more time and effort, if you didn't accept no for an answer, the problem would get solved. It would no longer be a problem.

As I reflect on my own leadership style, I have come to terms with the following: sometimes hard work alone won't get you where you want to go. As a leader, you have to be willing to quit, give your team permission to quit, pivot, and move forward together. When you hold onto *"Never Give Up"* and *"Just Stay Positive"* in the workplace and pretend you don't see or acknowledge the clear obstacles in the way, you are sowing the seeds of toxic positivity.

Consider the following questions:

- Are you someone who avoids conflict whenever possible? Would you rather brush off problems rather than deal with them directly?
- Would you rather hide your true feelings at work and rally behind feel-good mantras to get yourself and the team through the day?
- When other people's feelings make you uncomfortable, do you brush them off or minimize their feelings?
- Do you find yourself giving someone upbeat advice (*"everything happens for a reason,"* or *"it could be worse"*) rather than validating what they are feeling?
- Do you have a tough time quitting or accepting no as an answer? Are you concerned what others may think of you if you don't meet the goal you set out to achieve?
- Do you expect your team to be visibly happy at work and never bring their problems with them to the office?
- Do you consider individuals to be stirring up trouble and not be a team player when they identify problems arising at work?
- Do you believe if your team doesn't always look happy, upbeat, and positive, that this is a sign of you failing as a leader?

Avoiding becoming a bad boss, like the Cheerleader, involves being conscious of ourselves, recognizing our emotions and how we show up in the workplace. If you recognize yourself as someone spreading toxic positivity, it's time to stop. Aim for balancing and accepting positive and negative emotions and allowing your teams to do the same. If you are influenced by a boss or colleague who practices toxic positivity, it's time to set healthy boundaries and identify what you are willing to tolerate—or not.

What's the difference between a boss who is optimistic, practices positive thinking, coaches, and inspires their team and a bad boss who is just filled with toxic positivity?

Here are three things to watch out for to determine if you or someone on your team is embracing toxic positivity.

Bosses Who Surround Themselves with Yes People and Won't Take No for an Answer

"We won't take no for an answer," one sales leader I used to work with would always famously say. "*No* is not an option." This same sales leader surrounded himself with yes people, just like the Cheerleader did. People who did not challenge, push back, or question execution of recommendations that didn't make sense. This team consistently overpromised and underdelivered, quarter after quarter that I worked with them. The sales leader infected everyone around him with toxic positivity that conveyed anything was possible, even in the face of real business obstacles, shielding the whole team from reality.

In the few cases he was challenged, he would evoke military analogies and say, "Some of the greatest generals never retreated from the battlefield. We are staying on the field." He was always positive, smiling and upbeat when delivering his repetitive key messages, leaving many wondering if this behavior was harmful if he wasn't screaming and yelling.

An optimistic leader is balanced in positive thinking and being realistic. Good leaders inspire teams to push for more than they thought they could achieve. They are willing to hear about what's not working and roll up their sleeves and work with the team to problem-solve and quickly pivot. They know platitudes aren't going to help to change the reality. They will accept no and accept that indeed failure is an option. Once leaders accept failure, they can reevaluate what to do differently next time around.

Bosses Who Provide Excessive Compliments or Praise

A leader who is filled with toxic positivity may also shower others with excessive compliments to get them to do what needs to be done, just like the Cheerleader did to me. Even if the task at hand is not possible to complete or will cause an individual to sacrifice their physical and emotional well-being to get the work done. They will use praise, compliments, and flattery as forms of manipulation. They may appeal to someone's people-pleasing tendencies and need to come in to save the day, flattering them into doing what they would like done.

In a market where layoffs will continue, teams will be downsized and budgets will be cut. And often leaders won't make the tough calls on what work must stop and what work needs to continue. Individuals will be encouraged to do more with less resourcing, and sometimes it seems everything remains urgent. Toxic positivity can at first seem like a motivator, but over time can negatively affect team morale and productivity.

- Watch out for statements like these:

"You are the only person who can do this. You have such incredible expertise in this space. I just can't take you off this project."

"I know we have half the team members we used to have on this team, but you are strong enough to handle this workload. I believe in you!"

"You are superwoman! I am just so impressed with all the things you handle and juggle. I don't know how you do it all, and we are so lucky to have you on this team handling this urgent client issue."

> "I have never met anyone who thinks on their feet as quickly as you do! I am not worried at all about this launch under your leadership."
>
> "I know you can deliver this in two weeks with just some more hard work and perseverance. You'll sort through the challenges; you always do. You have never let me or the team down!"

A leader who is coaching their team will give "always-on" feedback, sharing the strengths and the areas of opportunities consistently. They won't weaponize positive feedback as a way to manipulate their team members into doing something that isn't possible. And if a task is indeed possible to complete, but the team member isn't able to complete it, the leader should sit down and give feedback on what they should focus on.

Bosses Who Expect People to Always Be Happy No Matter What the Circumstances

"Why aren't you smiling? What happened? Don't worry, be happy!" The Cheerleader would always say this to me, pointing to his mouth and making a hand gesture for me to smile.

And most of the time when I received this feedback, nothing had actually happened. I would be just at my desk diligently working, focused and apparently not smiling. But he wanted his team always smiling and always projecting happiness, no matter what the circumstances were.

In uncertain economic times, employees can feel overwhelmed at work by layoffs, hiring freezes, restructuring, controlling costs, colleagues resigning, and missing revenue targets. They can also feel overwhelmed by the increasing costs of childcare, natural disasters occurring in their communities, taking care of an elderly family member, and wars being waged around the world. It can be hard to always practice gratitude and be joyful at work. It can become an unreasonable demand and expectation from leaders.

When we pressure employees to erase how they are really feeling and put on a happy face, this can lead to burnout. After my last experience working for Medusa, when I was labeled a troublemaker and detractor, I stopped sharing my true feelings at work for some time. I buried my feelings while at the same time I felt like I was letting down my team.

Rather than practicing toxic positivity, leaders need to provide space to validate how team members are feeling. Leaders should avoid phrases like "It could be worse" and "Everything happens for a reason" and "Look at the bright side." Instead, actively listen and offer help and support. "I'm sorry this is happening. How can I help you today? Is there anything I can do for you at work to help support you?"

Do We Ask Women to Smile More Than Men?

I enjoy smiling. But when the Cheerleader would tell me to smile on demand, that's when I started to dislike smiling. And at times, I would shoot a quick smile back just to appease the situation. And I'm not alone in my experiences.

According to one study, 98% of women reported being told to smile at work sometime during the course of their careers.[6] 15% said the request to smile on demand happens weekly for them, if not more frequently. Of course, individuals who smile may be viewed as more happy, likable, and approachable. For women, smiling on demand in the workplace can seem more like a requirement. And for Black women, they can face sexism and racism in the workplace when they are labeled as "the angry Black woman."[7] According to *Harvard Business Review*, "This pervasive stereotype not only characterizes Black women as more hostile, aggressive, overbearing, illogical, ill-tempered

(continued)

(*continued*)

and bitter, but it may also be holding them back from real-izing their full potential in the workplace."[8]

"Smiling is very much associated as a gender marker," says Marianne LaFrance, a professor of women's, gender, and sexuality studies at Yale University and author of the book *Why Smile?*[9] "It marks one's femininity and a more communal stance toward life. Though smiling is generally a positive characteristic, it falls to women to do more of it because we want to make sure women are doing what we expect them to do, which is to care for others."

Telling women to smile may seem harmless in the workplace. And it reinforces the societal expectation that women should be cheerful, approachable, and make others feel more comfortable with a simple smile. So next time you ask a woman to smile at work, self-reflect on why she needs to smile to project that she's happy, confident, and contributing to the organization.

Remember that optimism and a positive mindset can strengthen our workplaces. However, leading with toxic positivity can backfire. The pressure for your team members to always be happy, have a can-do attitude, and persevere at any cost can be emotionally and physically exhausting. If we don't intervene and stop ourselves and others from becoming bad bosses like the Cheerleader, toxic positivity can be a key reason why employees move on from your company. And join a place where they don't have to pretend that everything is going to be okay, no matter what.

Tips for Leaders to Stop Promoting Toxic Positivity

- Start by self-reflecting and asking yourself if you are optimistic or full of toxic positivity.
- Remember the three things to watch out for to determine if you or someone on your team is embracing toxic positivity:
  - Bosses who surround themselves with yes people and won't take no for an answer:
    - An optimistic leader will be balanced in positive thinking and being realistic and accept no as a possibility.
  - Bosses who provide excessive compliments or praise:
    - A bad boss weaponizes positive feedback as a way to manipulate their team members into doing something that isn't possible.
  - Bosses who expect people to always be happy no matter what the circumstances:
    - Rather than practicing toxic positivity, leaders need to provide space to validate how team members are feeling.
- Reflect on whether or not you ask women to smile in the workplace more than men:
  - Why does a woman need to smile to project that she's happy, confident, and contributing to the organization?

10

The Boss Who Loved Gossiping . . . About Everyone

The Cheerleader, the Grinner, Medusa, and the Sheriff all had the following in common: working for each of them gave me flashbacks to the dreaded days of high school. Corporate America was the adult version of having to navigate the cliques, kiss up, avoid the bullies, find allies, and try to figure out where to sit at lunch when your work bestie called in sick (so they could Netflix binge all day).

And for most of us, that high school experience wasn't complete without the gossip. It was all about determining that social hierarchy and claiming status. Understanding the cliques and who was popular was important. Discussing what was happening in other students' personal lives was a way to establish your social status. Solidifying your position in the high school peck-ing order by using gossip to your advantage.

And in our workplaces, gossip can serve a similar purpose: a short cut to quickly increase your influence, status, and power.

Enter Gossip Girl.

I only worked for Gossip Girl for a brief period of time. And from the very day that she came to our division, I watched her flutter around the organization, from individual to individual, from team to team, gaining trust and gathering information. She saw every single interaction as a way to gather information, some-times information that didn't have anything to do with our actual work.

In the mornings, she was always in the kitchen with a black coffee, targeting her next source. She arrived 15 minutes early before the monthly town hall meetings to work the crowd and kiss up to management. She always had a glass of pinot noir in hand, lurking around the bar at every Thursday happy hour. She never ate lunch with the same person, always looking for a new companion to trade secrets with. She never missed a baby or a bridal shower or declined a wedding invite, showing up with extravagant gifts. Rather than focusing on doing actual work, Gossip Girl made it her full-time job to extract private, personal, or sensitive information. She wanted to be the first to know all the things very few knew or no one knew about at all.

Gossip Girl once told me that Nadia, our supply chain part-ner, was pregnant during one of our one-on-ones. But Nadia wasn't ready to announce it to the broader team; in fact, she herself was surprised to find out she was expecting. So, Gossip Girl leaned in, whispering the news in her office that had paper-thin walls. She asked me to keep that to myself. She said she trusted me with that confidential information.

Apparently, she also trusted seven other people on the team whom she also gossiped with about Nadia's pregnancy. Gossip Girl persuaded Nadia's boss to transition her to "less stressful" projects, using her pregnancy as a way to push Nadia out. This meant Gossip Girl could then work with her friend who was also in supply chain.

Gossip Girl told three of us on the team that the company had started a confidential search to replace the chief marketing officer. It was confidential, so the chief marketing officer didn't know he would be replaced next quarter. Gossip Girl was friends with one of the individuals on the executive recruiting team, she explained to us over lunch. We had to keep this a secret, of course. No one could find out.

The chief marketing officer found out about the secret. Because no one could keep the secret after Gossip Girl had confided the secret to a number of people. They had to exit him weeks earlier than they had originally planned. Gossip Girl was ready; she recommended a friend for the role who was ushered in quickly.

Gossip Girl told me over a coffee catch-up that Jason was really struggling in his new role. Jason was a peer to her, and it was no secret Gossip Girl didn't like him. She said that Jason didn't understand how the business model worked, got into a fight with the head of research and development, and also said that Jason was leaving the building for long periods of time because he was a smoker.

Jason confronted Gossip Girl one day in her office that had the paper-thin walls. "Why are you gossiping about me?" We could hear him say loudly. I had never heard anyone confront Gossip Girl about her gossiping ways until that day. I strained so hard to hear what she was saying in response but only heard very low murmurs.

"Stop gossiping about me," he said sternly, as he stormed out of the office a few minutes later. The door was open and I saw Gossip Girl frantically texting on her cell phone. I am sure she was quickly relaying to others what had just happened so she could control the narrative.

Jason knew his career was being sabotaged by Gossip Girl. And being new with few allies, there wasn't much he could do to stop her. He left the team about eight months after he started. Gossip Girl expanded her team, taking over Jason's responsibilities.

Gossip Girl also told us the only reason Jenna was promoted to the senior leadership team was because she was a woman. She told us Marc didn't leave to start a consulting business; he had a substance abuse problem. She gossiped about why Clarissa even worked since her husband was a hedge fund manager. She told us Tim cheated on his first wife with his now second wife (Tim and his current wife used to work together). She gossiped about our budgets being cut to fund the president's project to launch a premium granola bar and his college buddy was manufacturing the product.

"You know if Gossip Girl is gossiping about Marc and Clarissa, and pretty much the whole damn company, she's talking about us, too," a colleague whispered to me in the kitchen. I sipped my Earl Grey tea uncomfortably. I knew she was right.

For Gossip Girl, gossiping at work gave her a thrill. You could see the sparkle in her eyes and her mind racing. She was able to share something that wasn't public, and it could be completely unflattering information. She was like an investigative journalist who made her sources feel relaxed and comfortable. She went on to ask the probing questions—the *who, what, where, when,* and *why*—to get the information she needed. And unfortunately, she wasn't always good about protecting her sources.

"So do you think Riya is looking for a promotion? Do you think she's interviewing and trying to leave the team?"

"Umm . . . no . . ." I said, shifting uncomfortably in my seat. I caught myself on the receiving end of Gossip's Girl inquisition during a weekly one-on-one. I did not want to get involved. Riya was a friend.

"I mean, I don't know. Anyway, I wanted to chat about the forecast and . . ."

"You don't think she's ready for a promotion?" She interrupted me.

"No, that's not what I said . . ." I stumbled.

"Do you think she wants to leave the team?"

"I don't know . . . ." I stammered.

"Do you think I should promote her to keep her on the team?" She asked, leaning in.

"Yes, I think Riya has earned and deserves a promotion," I blurted out. "We all want to grow and advance in our careers and consider all options. Now, I really need to talk to you about the forecast for this product."

And I thought I had appeased Gossip Girl. That wasn't the end of it.

"Why would you tell her that I was interviewing?" A fuming Riya found me in the hallway the next day.

"Wait, what?" I said incredulously. "I never said that!"

"That's what she told me," Riya said. "She said you said I was interviewing to get off the team and get a better title."

"Riya, I never said that. Why would I say that?"

"I don't know," Riya said fighting back tears. "I thought we were friends. And now she knows I am interviewing. She says there aren't any promotion opportunities on this team so I should just leave if I want." Riya ran off to the bathroom before I could respond.

Gossip Girl didn't like that Riya and I were friends. So she tried to cause a rift between us (Riya didn't speak to me for a good three weeks after that incident). Gossip Girl used gossip to ruin relationships on her team that she thought might destabilize her career opportunities. She quietly chipped away at people's careers. She used gossip to try to advance her own standing in the company and cozy up to the executives, which she did rather successfully. In less than eight months, a board member helped her get a big title with a big pay increase in the external market. Gossip Girl moved on to continue gossiping elsewhere.

Years later, a former colleague from another job was interviewing with Gossip Girl. He shared the following exchange he had with Gossip Girl about me:

> "Did you ever work with Mita Mallick?"

That was about 15 minutes into the conversation. Gossip Girl was scanning his résumé and then putting dates and companies together and I guess, thought of me. Before he could answer, she continued on, "I never thought she was very good. Not very creative at all. I always wondered how she even got hired for that role." And then continued on with the interview.

My former colleague never acknowledged if he knew me or not. And he said he didn't want to work for a boss who gossiped, especially in an interview. He said it was a sure sign of a bad boss and only bad things to come. So he politely declined the offer.

★★★★

According to a UCLA study, everyone gossips. The researchers defined gossip as "simply talking about someone who isn't present. That talk could be positive, neutral, or negative."[1] The study also revealed the following:[2]

- On average, people gossip about 52 minutes per day.
- Women and men tend to gossip about the same amount.
- Extroverts gossip far more frequently than introverts, across all three types of gossip.

People love to talk about people. Gossip has been found to help strengthen social bonds between individuals.[3] It's a way for people to understand themselves and each other. It's a way to exchange information, vent emotions, and entertain ourselves. As long as we have workplaces, we will have individuals gossiping. And gossiping in the workplace, as I saw firsthand with my former boss, can also have a dark side.

Workplace gossip can become dangerous. Particularly if the boss is the one who constantly blabbers, is unable to keep secrets, starts or spreads rumors, talks too much, weaponizes confidential information, and just simply gossips indiscreetly. A bad boss constantly gossiping can result in the following:

- Loss of trust among the team; it can divide team members, leaving individuals to question whom to believe and wondering potentially what side to take
- Increased anxiety if team members feel pressured to gossip with the boss, try to make sense of why this information is being shared, and wonder if they may be the next target of gossip
- Loss of productivity as team members get sucked into the gossip
- Significant negative impact on team members' careers and their well-being
- Increased resignations with individuals tired of a gossiping boss creating a toxic work environment

When individuals operate in silos and there is a lack of transparent communication, gossip can be on the rise. When the boss is the one gossiping about others, they role model that it's okay for others to gossip. The bad boss may even encourage it. And they will be unknowingly or knowingly creating the next generation of Gossip Girls in the workplace.

Are You Gossip Girl?

I would be lying if I said I have never gossiped during the course of my career. I am embarrassed to admit I have been pressured into gossiping with former bosses like the Gossip Girl. Early on in my career when other colleagues made fun of me for being too nice, and never saying anything bad about anyone, I would sit and listen to them laugh about others, trying to "to fit in." Having been the target of harmful gossip at work, I now know firsthand the damage it can have on one's career.

And yet why do so many of us still gossip? Even when we are the boss and "in charge"?

Consider the following questions:

- Do you find yourself feeling insecure at work, especially when you compare yourself to other leaders? Do you look for information to position yourself to be perceived as better than them? Even if that information hurts them but makes you look good?
- Do you feel like when you are "in the know" you are then part of the team? Do you use gossip, particularly confidential or sensitive information, as a way to get into the inner circle at work? To get closer to senior leadership?
- Do you find you have meaningful connections with others at work where you talk about positive things? Or are most of your closest connections at work centered on harmful gossip?
- Do you find yourself being drawn to gossip about team members who aren't performing, aren't capable or confident? Do you avoid giving them direct feedback on their performance?

■ Have you ever been the target of harmful gossip in the workplace? How did that make you feel?

■ How would you feel if your boss or colleagues were gossiping about you and saying things that weren't true?

We may not set out to be mean when we gossip. And if we can't uncover why we gossip, we can't stop the behavior. When we become Gossip Girl, gossiping negatively about others, we cause harm. Bad bosses erode trust and inclusion. They can also do harm to someone's reputation and ultimately cause damage to the team and the entire organization.

Here are three ways you can ensure you and your teams put an end to harmful gossiping.

Stop and Pause Before Gossiping

Before you open your mouth to gossip, stop and pause. Ask yourself the following:

■ Are you gossiping to get ahead at work? Will this benefit you and hurt someone else?

■ Are you stretching the truth? Are you distorting information? Are you exaggerating to make the story more appealing?

■ Are you throwing someone under the bus or stabbing someone in the back?

■ Are you sharing something that is negative about someone else?

■ Will this information damage someone else's reputation?

- Are you reporting something as facts without having confirmation of whether it's true or not?
- What happens if you share this news? Who will be negatively affected?

While you may be tempted to gossip in the moment or find yourself being lured by others to join in the gossiping, think before you contribute anything. Don't contribute to workplace drama by spreading misinformation or sharing news that's not for you to share. And remember, as a boss, when you speak, your words carry a lot of weight, whether you realize it or not.

Don't Engage in Gossip

If bad bosses like the Gossip Girl and others are trying to get you to join in the gossip, don't engage. If they keep pressuring you to add fuel to the fire, put an end to it. Here are some phrases to consider using (and adjust depending on the situation):

- Let's not share this information with others when we don't have all the facts.
- If you are concerned about what happened last week, let's make sure we discuss it at our weekly team meeting when we are all there instead of having multiple one-on-one conversations.
- I don't know Mita or anything about this situation. I have nothing to add.
- I recommend you go and speak to Mita directly about what you just shared with me.
- Honestly, I don't feel comfortable that we are talking about Mita and she's not here. I would be upset if someone was talking about me without me knowing about it.
- Mita is not here to defend herself. Why don't you directly ask her what happened?

We have to do more than just not engage in the gossip. We can't stay silent. We also have a responsibility to stop and shut gossip down when it happens right in front of us.

Set a Culture of Transparent Communication

Gossip can't grow and thrive in cultures where we have transparent communication. When individuals feel insecure, uncertain, or are siloed on our teams, gossip will start. Consider the following ways to set a culture where everyone feels like they are part of the team, so there's no need for gossip:

- Be as transparent as possible about the challenges and opportunities the organization faces, the wins and the losses, especially in uncertain economic times so gossip doesn't start to swirl about what may or may not happen. It's okay to share that you have no further information at this time and will update the team as soon as you can.
- Make sure your words match your actions. Don't say you are transparent and then have side conversations with certain team members and keep information from others. Be consistently transparent, not just selectively transparent or transparent only when it's convenient.
- Include team members in decision-making when appropriate. And if you make a decision counter to what they recommended or make it on your own without their inputs, explain your rationale. If you make decisions in hiding and don't bring your team along, it's likely gossiping will start.
- Take accountability for your mistakes and have your team's back when they make mistakes. Coach your team through mistakes rather than pointing fingers and placing blame. Be open about mistakes with the team so everyone can learn from them.

- Let team members know where they stand. Insecurity about where we stand in terms of our performance can breed gossip, so be generous with feedback. Celebrate their efforts and acknowledge their hard work. Be open and honest when someone isn't meeting expectations. As we discussed, don't wait to intervene when it comes to actively disengaged team members. Coach them and guide them. If this team or organization isn't where they are meant to be, help them move forward to their next opportunity.

- Remember that there is no place in our organizations for individuals actively and repeatedly hurting and harming others. When gossip starts to spread like wildfire about these individuals, it's likely because leadership hasn't intervened. These bad bosses are often the worst-kept secrets in our organizations.

- Listen when people share their concerns and believe their experiences. When team members feel that they are seen and heard by their leader, they are less likely to gossip.

- Provide real opportunities for team members to build meaningful relationships, not just based on gossip. Ensure they are working together on cross-functional projects. Give them a stipend for breakfast or lunch outings. Ask them how they would like to bond outside of work in activities that everyone feels comfortable participating in.

- Finally, create a culture where team members want to spread positive and accurate information about each other, lifting and supporting each other whenever possible:
  - "Mita got promoted! I am so excited for her and it's well deserved."
  - "Lan's team won the beauty industry award! They just announced the winners."

- "Dinah is presenting her recommendation to the CEO next week! She's going to nail it!"
- "Kevin was selected to go to the leadership conference. Such great news!"
- "Unfortunately, Damon's role was eliminated. And great news, he found a role on another team, so he's staying!"

As long as workplaces exist, gossip will exist. Because people enjoy talking about people. And a work culture seeped in gossip can become toxic, particularly when it's the boss who is the one gossiping. The power of gossiping cannot be underestimated. We can start to create silos, individuals start choosing and picking sides, and suddenly rumors and misinformation are more believable and carry more weight than public announcements from the leaders of the company. And finally, the damage done to those who are the target of gossiping can have an incredibly negative impact on their careers and ultimately their overall well-being.

So just shut the gossiping down.

No one wants to feel like they are trapped in an episode of *Gossip Girl* in their workplaces.

Particularly if the boss is the one who can't keep their mouth shut.

Tips for Stopping Harmful Gossip in Our Workplaces

- Accept that most people like to gossip and watch out for the signs when it can become hurtful or harmful in our workplaces.
- Self-reflect on whether as the boss you are gossiping and why that might be.
- Acknowledge and understand the impact a boss gossiping can have on the broader team. Remember your words carry weight.
- Focus on these three ways you can ensure you and your teams put an end to harmful gossiping:
  - Stop and pause before gossiping. Ask yourself why you want to spread this information, what your true intentions are, and the impact it could have.
  - Don't engage. You also have a responsibility to stop and shut gossip down when it happens right in front of you.
  - Set a culture of transparent communication. Gossip can't grow and thrive in cultures where you have transparent communication.

11

The Boss Who Loved the Spotlight and Took Credit for *All* of the Work

After Gossip Girl said goodbye to the team, I let out a big sigh of relief. I survived yet another bad boss. I went on to get promoted, led bigger teams, and switched business functions. As I got more senior, I thought I would get better, become more astute at detecting bad boss behavior.

And I was naive in thinking that the more senior you were, the less likely you were to be a bad boss. In some cases, if you had never parted with these bad boss behaviors, they grew with you as you grew your career. And bad boss behaviors became harder and harder to shed over time.

While I was quick to recognize a multitude of bad boss behaviors, there was one obvious behavior I had yet to truly experience.

Enter Spotlight.

Not only did this bad boss love being the center of attention, he loved taking credit for all of our work. And I mean all of it. Down to every single last sentence, grammatical mistakes and all.

Similar to the Grinner, he had failed up. He had sweet-talked his way (without using any malicious gossip) into leading a very large US division after having just finished an assignment in Brazil. While he didn't know how to do much, he did have some key skills: he was fantastic at socializing and making strangers suddenly his best friends; he was very astute in gaining access to the power brokers in the organization; he was great at memorizing facts, figures, and lines he didn't understand the meaning of. I always thought he would have made a terrific actor. Yet he chose the corporate stage to make his mark.

Spotlight loved being on the podium, stage, stand, high-riser—quite frankly anything with an elevated platform. A close colleague and friend had chosen his brilliant nickname. Because like a moth to a flame, he was immediately drawn to the warm, bright lights. (And you just couldn't get him away from the lights no matter what.) He loved giving speeches just about anywhere: impromptu gatherings in the cafeteria, team stand-up meetings in his office, long-winded and rambling speeches at a team off-site. And if there was no podium, he would stand up on a chair.

He loved accepting a shiny, glass, or any type of metal award, or a heavy framed certificate. He enjoyed a good ribbon-cutting ceremony, where of course he got to pose cutting the ribbon followed by thunderous applause. He preferred a mic clipped to his collared shirt versus a handheld mic because he was a hand talker; his hands flew every which way while speaking. His social media feed was all pictures of him doing what he loved doing:

being in the limelight, front and center, and basking in the spotlight.

Of course, he enjoyed taking credit for all of our work in the glow of warm lights when he had an audience. He also equally enjoyed stealing, copying, cutting and pasting, lifting, and plagiarizing our work. He didn't want to do any work but was more than happy to present our work as his own.

Spotlight would forward me emails saying, "Can you send your thoughts?"

The email was typically from his boss or the CEO asking Spotlight's thoughts on a way forward on a project, a recent competitive move, or a potential acquisition target. Of course, I would quickly write back a well-crafted email with my feedback. One time, he accidentally forwarded an email chain back to me where I discovered he was directly cutting and pasting my responses and presenting them as his own ideas.

Spotlight asked us to create every document and every deck the leadership team ever requested. I filled out the talk track on every slide for him. We had dress rehearsals where he would recite back to us every single thing we had told him. We sat there nodding our heads and listening as if what he was sharing was so profound and as if we were hearing it for the very first time.

When I once asked if I and other team members could present, he said "Okay, sure. You all can speak to slides 7–10." Then mysteriously he never invited us to the meeting. This happened on a number of occasions. I finally stopped asking because I realized that he just couldn't bear to share the spotlight.

Spotlight asked me to send unsolicited notes to his boss saying how great he was. And this was the only time I ever saw him give someone else credit for his work. He would tell me what to write, what to emphasize, or sometimes even write it himself. He would then ask me to forward that email back to him so he could confirm that I had sung his praises to his boss.

Spotlight copied our performance reviews. He would call and ask me to send my self-evaluation in advance of putting it in the system. I wondered why that was. He would then do a follow-up call and ask me for more specific data and numbers on various projects I was leading. And I then found out he did this to other people on the team. One time, his executive assistant, instead of sending out the quarterly business review deck, sent out Spotlight's self-evaluation to the team. I opened it and scanned the document. He did what he was always so good at doing, lifting every single line and statistic, even down to the exact word and punctuation mark.

Spotlight was once terribly upset that he couldn't be on a big Manhattan stage to accept an award on behalf of the company. Our new CEO was available to come to the ceremony and was accepting the award. "But she just got here," he complained and whined to me like one of my kids do when I take away the iPad. "It's not fair when we did all the work."

"Well," I replied, completely baffled. "She is the CEO after all."

Days later, he proudly showed up with the award in our monthly team meeting. He must have gotten the award from the CEO's assistant. He said it was like our Stanley cup moment. It was a heavy, glass award. He suddenly held it up high in the air, like a scene out of *Lion King* with Simba being raised to the blue skies with "The Circle of Life" soundtrack playing in my head. He then dramatically kissed the award.

He passed it around the room. No mention of the work my team and I had done to get the company this recognition. I looked at the award with the smudge mark of his lips still there and shuddered. I quickly passed it along.

Afterwards, he put the award carefully away in his black leather messenger bag. Days, weeks, and months later, I never saw that award in the lobby where all of our company awards were prominently displayed. My colleagues and I suspected that he took it home and placed it on his fireplace mantel. I bet that glass award with the smudge mark of his lips is still there above a roaring fire.

That spring, a massive hurricane hit the area with flooding everywhere. The offices were closed, and we all worked from home for the week. During that time, he had me preparing detailed slides for a board meeting on an urgent topic. The board didn't care about the flooding in New York; they were meeting in Paris where the sun was shining and there wasn't a drop of rain. So I was working and working and working. Both my kids were at home and my husband was typing away in the next room. We took shifts to watch our kids waiting for the schools to reopen.

After hours of toiling away on the deck, I finally decided to take a 30-minute lunch break. I stepped away from both the laptop and the phone. I plopped down on the couch eating the kids' leftover peanut butter sandwiches. When I headed back to my laptop and phone, I had over half a dozen missed calls and Microsoft Teams messages. Spotlight was on the hunt for me. I took a deep breath and called him back.

"Where were you?" He shouted at me. "We need those slides finished by this afternoon."

"I was eating lunch."

There was silence on the other end.

Then he shouted, "I don't know if you realize this, Mita. But THIS, this is our moment to SHINE."

I almost busted out laughing, tried to hold it in, and snorted loudly instead into the phone.

"Are you okay?" He asked, startled as he heard the loud snort.

"Oh, yes, just a bad cough," I said, adding in a fake cough for good measure. "I'll get those slides over to you in the next hour."

I heard that board meeting went very, very well. So well, in fact, that it was part of what helped Spotlight to get promoted again, to another job that was too big for him. And lucky for him, he had another big brand-new team ready and waiting to do all the work.

"So he got promoted off all of your hard work," my mother said, annoyed, wrinkling her nose. I was updating her over FaceTime on what was happening at work. I laughed in response, because otherwise I would have cried. Even my mom knew what was up.

Years later, I saw Spotlight at a conference. I avoided making contact and spotted him from afar. There he was on a panel on stage. Right under the warm bright lights talking with his hands in the air. Some bad bosses just never seem to change.

★★★★★★

According to a Korn Ferry survey, nearly 50% of respondents say their boss has taken credit for the work they did.[1] The survey also found that 56% of individuals said their boss motivates them very little or not at all, which isn't surprising if they are not being credited for the impact they are having at work.[2] And 40% of individuals said they could "do their boss's job better than their manager."[3] I would argue it's not that they *could do* their boss's job better; it's that in most cases they *already are* in fact doing their boss's job.

When it comes to the boss taking credit for an individual's or the team's work, I have heard a litany of excuses as to why this continues to happen in our workplaces. Over the years, leaders I have worked with and coached have rationalized and justified the stealing of someone else's work with the following statements:

> "Listen, it's our job to make our bosses look great."
> "Well, the CEO asked me and only me to present, so that's not my fault."

"This new generation is a bunch of whiners. That's what bosses do; that's what my boss always did."
"This is a team effort. There is no *I* in *team*."
"This is just how this place works. No one ever gets to present their work."

In school, when we copy someone else's homework, cheat on a test, or plagiarize a paper, there are consequences. They may send us to the principal's office and call our parents. We may receive a written warning. We may fail the test. We may fail the class. We may be suspended for the day. Depending on the type of cheating that has occurred, and if this behavior continues, we can be expelled from school. There are anti-cheating pledges, honor codes, academic integrity committees, and more. While we are taught in school from a young age not to cheat, we graduate and enter our workplaces where taking credit for other people's work seems to be a given perk when we become the boss. And bad bosses like Spotlight build the entire success of their careers not on what they did, but on what others did.

"It's amazing what you can accomplish if you do not care who gets credit" is a quote attributed to Harry S Truman.[4] Many of us have been taught to strive for the greater good of the team in our careers. Bad bosses will take advantage of an individual's desire to be a team player, collaborate, and do whatever it takes to pitch in, as long as it helps the team and overall goal. They enjoy holding onto and spreading the myth of "it doesn't matter who gets credit."

Here's the question we should all be asking: How can leaders fairly evaluate individuals if they don't know what their specific contributions are?

Because when it comes to year-end performance reviews, most of the focus is on the individual performance, and not on how the team did overall. Leaders want to be able to understand how someone stood out, what their unique contributions were, and the size of individual impact. I have rarely heard a leader give someone an outstanding performance review with only the feedback "great teamwork!"

Do You Give Individuals on Your Team Credit for Their Work?

Just like cheating in school, we may take credit from others on our teams, cheat, or steal their work for similar reasons: we are afraid to fail, we lack confidence in our capabilities, or we don't understand what to do. We may lack planning skills and wait until the last minute to deliver something, or just aren't motivated to do it. We may delegate this work to someone on our team and take their work and present it as our own. Unfortunately, when enough bosses do this in our workplaces, this bad boss behavior can become normalized.

So are you the good leader who gives others credit for their work? Or are you veering toward the path of becoming the bad boss who loves the spotlight?

Consider the following questions:

- How often do you let your team present their own work? Often? Occasionally? Never?
- How do you think your team would respond to the first question?
- Can you recall a specific time in the last month or last quarter when individuals on your team shared their own work? How often did you speak versus letting them have airtime?
- Do you let your team share ideas, documents, and decks with your own boss directly? Or do you serve as the middle person, sharing their work with your boss? Do

you let your boss know it's your team's work, or do you just let them assume you did the work?

- How many of your former bosses gave you credit for your contributions? How many of your bosses were credit thieves?
- Do you worry that if you aren't always the one presenting, sharing, and talking that others will wonder what you do as a leader?
- Were you taught that your number-one job was to make your boss look good? Do you expect, now that you are the boss, that your team should do all the work and you get the credit? Because that's how it has always been done?

Bad bosses steal ideas, take credit, and save the spotlight for themselves. Good leaders give others credit for their work, share the limelight, and sometimes even move off the stage when they know it's someone else's turn to be front and center.

Receiving credit and being recognized for the impact we are having at work is key to feeling included in the workplace. While the marketplace is filled with advice on how to navigate a bad boss taking credit for your work, we don't discuss enough how to stop these credit thieves in the first place. Here are three questions to ask ourselves to ensure as leaders we give our team members the credit and recognition they deserve, and stop others and ourselves from hogging the spotlight.

Do You Know What Every Team Member Is Specifically Working On?

If you have a bad boss like Spotlight working for you, chances are they don't want you to know what their team members work on. If they are taking credit for their work, they will try to keep you as far away from the team as possible. My former boss did everything he could to stop me or anyone else on the team from developing any kind of relationship with his boss.

Ask yourself the following when you think of your broader team:

- Do you know at least one thing they are working on?
- Do you know who develops creative and differentiated ideas?
- Do you know who is on track to exceed their targets or goals?
- Do you know who is launching and executing projects successfully?
- Do you know who is stepping in to help on other projects?

Depending on the size of the broader team, consider the following to bypass a bad boss who takes all the credit in order to get access to team members:

- Ask for skip-level meetings so you can meet with your team members' direct reports a few times a year.
- Strive to build independent relationships with team members in addition to skip-level meetings; stop by their desks on the way to a meeting, send them a message to check in, seek them out to say hello at team gatherings.
- Create a simple quarterly exercise where you ask everyone on the team to send you two sentences sharing what they are working on that they are most proud of.

Knowing what team members are working on is a key first step to ensure they get credit and the recognition they deserve.

Do You Give Team Members Opportunities to Step into the Spotlight?

There's no denying hierarchies exist in our workplaces. There are times only certain people can attend meetings, only certain people can present, only certain people can speak. This is an opportunity as leaders to break those hierarchies in our workplaces, to challenge and ask ourselves why we don't let team members share and present their own work.

This is also an opportunity to think of other ways to share the spotlight across the team:

- Invite team members to share what they are working on at monthly or quarterly team meetings. Keep the request simple: one standard slide or no slides at all with a brief update on an initiative they are leading. Ensure you rotate who gets to share.
- Offer opportunities to attend workshops, conferences, award dinners, and more across the team. Allow everyone a chance to attend something on behalf of the company as also a way to acknowledge and thank them for their efforts.
- Ask for peer nominations to highlight team members and their contributions. You can create categories like "Best problem-solver" or "Focuses on customer excellence" or "Goes the extra mile." You can ask peers to include a brief description of why they are nominating this person. Share these nominations either in a reoccurring team meeting, in a company newsletter, or any venue or vehicle to spotlight their work.

Don't use the excuse of corporate hierarchy to keep individuals out of the spotlight and keep them behind the scenes when it comes to sharing their own work.

Do You Create a Culture Where You Recognize Team Members' Contributions?

When we role model positive behavior as leaders, we help set the foundation for great team cultures. That means as leaders, we can't be credit thieves or idea stealers. Another former boss used to say to me "Let me borrow your genius" or "Can I pick your brain today" to mine me for ideas and pass them off as his own. When we as leaders normalize that it's acceptable to take credit for other people's ideas and work, we sow the seeds for a culture where bad bosses like Spotlight thrive. By allowing for bad bosses like this to win at work, we encourage the next generation of bosses to adopt these terrible behaviors.

As leaders, we have a responsibility to ensure everyone has an opportunity to own their work on our teams. Consider statements like the following, and adapt them to your own language and adjust depending on the context:

- "Mita, feel free to kick off the presentation at next week's meeting. Then I would love for you to turn it over to Zachary and Lily, who did the customer analysis."
- "Mita, appreciate you sharing the project recommendation. Can you also let me know who else was involved in this work? I believe it was Priya, Emma, and Julia? Am I missing anyone else?"
- "Mita, since you presented at the last town hall, I would love for Jay to have the opportunity to present on behalf of the team."

When you set the example by creating a culture where everyone is given credit and recognized for their work, that positive behavior can spread like wildfire. You will find individuals shifting from stealing and taking credit to wanting to give and share credit. Let's make it impossible for bad bosses like Spotlight to thrive, let alone survive, in our workplaces.

During the course of our careers, most of us will work for some version of a bad boss like Spotlight. It can slowly chip away at our self-confidence and self-worth. Because when we come to work, we want to know that what we do matters. And that we are recognized for our contributions. Having someone consistently steal our ideas and take credit for our work can make us feel like we are slowly being erased on our teams. Especially when that person is our boss and holds significant power over our careers in that moment that we work for them. While we may not always have the power to stop our bosses from being credit thieves, we do have the power to break the cycle. To stop hogging those warm bright lights. To step to the right to make room for others and share that spotlight.

Tips for Ensuring Team Members Get Credit and Recognition for Their Work

- Do you give individuals on your team credit for their work?
  - Are you the leader who gives others credit for their work? Or are you veering toward the path of becoming the bad boss who loves the spotlight?
- Do you know what every team member is specifically working on?
  - Knowing what team members are working on is a key first step to ensure they get credit and the recognition they deserve.
- Do you give team members opportunities to step into the spotlight?
  - Think of ways to spotlight team members across the team.
- Do you create a culture where you recognize team members' contributions?
  - Lead by example and ensure everyone is given credit and recognized for their work so this positive behavior can spread like wildfire through your team.
- Finally, if you are looking for more specific guidance on how to be a more inclusive leader who ensures everyone's voice matters and is heard on your teams, please check out my first book, *Reimagine Inclusion: Debunking 13 Myths to Transform Your Workplace.*

12

The Boss Who Questioned My Loyalty and Called Me a Rat

Like many of you, I have experienced a wide range of bad bosses.

I had to learn to survive three of the worst, most dreadful, and at times most horrific bosses I ever had in my career. And I promised myself I would do everything I could to never, ever become any one of those three bad bosses.

First, there was the Sheriff who did not want to learn how to say my full first name Madhumita, or call me Mita, and so he decided to nickname me Mohammed.

Second, there was Medusa, who had temper tantrums like a toddler, throwing pens and even once her Chanel shoe at a colleague.

And there was Tony. Tony Soprano. With one swift phone call, he could kill someone's career.

Tony might just be the worst boss I ever had. And one of the best boss nicknames I ever came up with (even my husband agrees).

Enter Tony.

Tony Soprano is a fictional character who rises in the ranks to become the mob boss of the fictional DiMeo crime family of North Jersey, in the series *The Sopranos*.[1] Tony is a complex character, portrayed as a family man attending his children's school events and having dinner with his wife. He's also abusive and violent. He's a calculating and ruthless mob boss who is on a quest for power and control at all costs.

The first time I met my former boss Tony was at a well-known Italian restaurant in the city. He was courting me for a role on his team. During that first lunch, he was loud and bombastic, quiet and reflective, and he was utterly charming. He smiled a lot, shared hilarious stories from his time climbing the corporate ladder, made me feel important, and exuded an air of confidence, with a slight hint of arrogance.

"It's a one-year assignment, 12 months," Tony explained about the offer he was making. "Then you can go back to running one of the biggest brands. The CEO and I agreed, you will have your pick after this year."

The offer seemed too good to pass up, so I took it. Little did I know, once you were part of Tony's organization, you didn't get to leave. Until he said you could.

Tony's charm quickly melted away after I joined the team. Unlike Medusa, he didn't showcase his temper in public. He was cool, calm, and in control as he walked the hallways. And the first time he asked me to give him feedback about how he delivered a presentation was when I saw the other side. He growled and shouted because I offered my honest feedback, which he had asked for. He said in response that I was "one of the worst presenters" he had ever seen. I then found myself in a women's bathroom stall, quietly sobbing, as I had done so many times at the beginning of my career.

Tony, similar to my former boss the Sheriff, kept a network of people close to him. They fed him information so he could keep a tight grip on the team. He never gossiped with this information. Unlike the Sheriff, Tony had the power to end careers at the company. One morning he found out our colleague Harry was interviewing for a role externally. By that afternoon, Harry was meeting with human resources (HR). His role had been eliminated; he was escorted out by security. The external role Harry was interviewing for disappeared. Tony had gotten to the hiring manager, who was at another company.

Tony had given me a sign-on bonus when joining. Three months later, it had yet to hit my bank account. I was scared to ask Tony and hoped the money would appear. My husband kept reminding me this was money I had earned. I delicately approached the topic at the end of one of our one-on-ones.

"Why are you asking me about this? You don't trust me? You don't think you will get it?" He peppered me with questions, as he scrolled through his phone, not making eye contact.

"I was only asking . . ." I stammered. "Because . . ."

"You will be taken care of."

His assistant then came and ushered me out of his office. I was too scared to ask again. The sign-on bonus finally appeared in my account five months after it was promised.

Tony once called us into a conference room to review our team employee engagement survey results. Some team members had made the mistake of giving honest feedback about his leadership style. While HR said it was confidential, that didn't mean it was anonymous. Tony was able to track down who said what. I shuddered and was grateful I had submitted nothing. He rattled off feedback: "He's unhinged during our one-on-ones" and "threatens my job routinely" and "he's a sociopath who needs help and should be terminated immediately." He made intense eye contact with who had said what, without ever making an accusation.

"I'm going to forgive you and let all this go," he said calmly. "Family sticks together. Next time you have an issue, come to me, not someone outside of this family."

In the weeks to follow, each family member who had given the most devastating feedback about Tony was put on a performance improvement plan. They were exited one by one by one that year.

Tony called me a rat. During our one-on-one meeting, I made him aware that another team was working on the same confidential initiative we were working on. At this point, I was eight months into the role, almost at the finish line. I thought providing him information would get me in his good graces and make these last four months bearable. He turned the tables on me.

Tony leaned back in his chair and looked at me, "I smell a rat in here."

Since the building had just been renovated and was experiencing rodent issues, I thought a rat died in his office. I got up startled, looking around. "You smell a rat?"

"I smell a rat."

I didn't know how to respond.

"I said, I smell a rat, Mita."

I suddenly realized what he was saying.

"What?" I blurted out. "I wouldn't say anything to anyone about Project Restart. Why would I share something confidential?"

"At this point, I am not sure who to trust anymore. There's a rat and I am going to find it."

I left his office stunned and confided in a team member while we were in the women's bathroom about what had happened. This was the only place we knew Tony wouldn't enter but I still had to be careful who may be listening in.

"I'm resigning tomorrow," she grabbed my hands and begged me not to tell anyone. "You need to get out."

"I'm leaving soon, I'm almost at my eight-month mark," I reassured her. "I'll be done after my year."

"Oh, Mita, he's not going to let you go."

She was right.

In the beginning of December, on a Tuesday afternoon, Tony texted me, called me, and emailed me incessantly within a 15-minute time frame. I was at a baby shower lunch celebrating one of my colleagues. I had put my phone away to enjoy my soup. My stomach dropped as I looked at the screen.

"Mita, you should come back to the office," his assistant had messaged.

I drove back with my mind racing on what could have happened. I collected myself, calmly walked into his office, said hello, and shut the door.

"So, I hear you are trying to leave the team," he stated.

"I'm not sure . . ."

"Did you or did you not have conversations with other leaders about moving to their teams? Behind my back? Without telling me?" he began raging, slowly becoming unhinged.

"I didn't go behind your back," I said, trying to get him to calm down. "We agreed that this would be a 12-month assignment, so I have been meeting with other leaders to get their advice."

"Oh, this is at least a two- to four-year assignment," he continued to rail. "You haven't even begun to make an impact."

"But you said it was one year and then I could . . ."

"You leave this team when I SAY you can LEAVE," he bellowed at me. "I DECIDE when you leave."

He took a sip of his water and then said matter-of-factly, "Besides, no one wants you on their team. That's what they all tell me. You are lucky to have a job at this company."

He went back to typing on his laptop as if I wasn't even sitting there. I sat there, looking at him. I got up and left.

That was the day I went home and started another "get-out" spreadsheet to map out my escape plan. I knew staying internally wouldn't be an option; Tony's reach was far and wide, and he would do his best to destroy my career even if I stayed. I carefully crafted my exit strategy, reaching out to people externally who had once had to endure Tony's wrath for help. Because if you had ever worked or crossed paths with Tony, you had an immediate bond even if you had never met. A bad boss like Tony can actually create strong bonds among individuals who are trying to defeat or avoid being killed by a common enemy.

I told one close friend and colleague at work I was looking to escape, someone who provided endless hours of moral support. I played the game, kept smiling, kept nodding, kept working. Never once did I raise flags that I was unhappy or wanted to leave without Tony's permission. I needed to channel every single acting skill I had in me. Because I was on a singular mission to get out and I wouldn't, I couldn't let Tony stop me.

It took me longer than I wanted, and eventually I was able to make that phone call to tell him I was leaving. He was at a conference and avoiding my calls. I finally got him on the phone. I let him know I was putting in my two weeks' notice.

"After everything I have done for you? After all the kindness I have showed you?" he shouted into the phone.

He kept on railing. And ranting. He wouldn't stop. He was once again, unhinged.

I finally interrupted him.

"This is no longer a productive conversation. Have a good weekend."

And I hung up.

When I left, there was no announcement, there was no party, no card, no gift. Because I had left Tony. I had crossed him. I had no loyalty. I had betrayed him. He painted the narrative that I was the villain, the traitor, and the troublemaker, and continued those stories long after I left. And as I healed from that experience, I became comfortable and content in being the villain in Tony's stories. Because when it comes to bad bosses, sometimes the only way to get out from under their reign is to become the villain in their story. Sometimes, it's the only way to save yourself and reclaim your own story again.

★★★★★

When it comes to loyalty in our workplaces, many of us were raised with the romantic vision of what work once was: our parents' and grandparents' daily commute to the same workplace year after year to give their families a better life. They were valued and their contributions mattered. Their jobs were secure. They knew they would be taken care of as long as they showed up not just for their companies, but more importantly for their bosses, too.

Today, employee loyalty looks very different. According to one study, the average person will change their jobs 12 times over the course of their career, which shows that job hopping is become increasingly more common, particularly in tough economic times.[2] The average employee will stay at their employer for 4.3 years;[3] gone are the days of collecting a shiny gold Rolex to commemorate 30 years of service. And apparently after one bad day at work, 45% of employees who had been at their companies for less than a year said they had applied for a new job.[4] These bad days at work don't just mysteriously happen; we know that bad bosses can play an outsized role in creating those bad days, which can lead to saying "I quit!"

In *The End of Loyalty: The Rise and Fall of Good Jobs in America*, author Rick Wartzman details the erosion of the relationship between US corporations and employees.[5] He shares how big businesses once took responsibility for providing for their employees, creating a corporate social contract: companies provided job security and employees in return had unwavering loyalty. Over time, this social contract was broken. Downsizing, globalization, outsourcing, the rise of artificial intelligence, and instability now means that job security, steadily rising pay, and health benefits are not guaranteed. So how can we believe that loyalty should be a given from our employees?

I have worked with so many leaders who still expect loyalty, no matter what:

- "Mita went behind my back, sharing 'her career aspirations' with other team leaders."
- "He must be in this role three years. He has some nerve to be asking me about promotion timelines."
- "Everyone needs to be in the office five days a week, I don't care how long your commute is. Let's see who is really loyal and committed."
- "Did you see this résumé? They were only at their last job for two years."
- "Why does this new generation have zero loyalty? It's not how I was raised."

Like my former boss Tony, these bad bosses don't believe they play any role in having to earn or win the loyalty of their teams. These bad bosses believe they completely own individuals' careers: they decide and dictate who gets to leave their team when and why. If you challenge their authority in any way, they have serious doubts about your commitment to them and to the company. And because you get a paycheck every two weeks, that's the price in exchange for your loyalty. No questions asked.

Do You Demand Loyalty, or Do You Try to Earn Loyalty?

Most of us won't try to intimidate and threaten our team members, demanding loyalty from them at all costs like my former bad boss Tony. And yet many of us need to answer this: Do we demand loyalty or do we try to earn loyalty? Because the answer to that question can be the tipping point of whether we start to fall into bad boss territory. Consider the following questions:

- Do you expect your team members to be loyal and committed to you because they are getting a paycheck?
- Do you believe team members should wait their turn when it comes to promotion and advancement opportunities?
- Do you get aggravated when they ask you about a promotion timeline or ask to have their compensation reviewed? Do you believe they should trust you to take care of them?
- Do you believe that you are in charge of your team member's career and what they do next?
- Do you feel insecure or jealous when you hear your team member reaching out to others for career advice?
- Do you feel betrayed when someone resigns or moves off your team?
- Do you cut former team members off once they have left your team?
- Do you find yourself using "the family" analogy to ensure everyone has a strong sense of loyalty to you?
- What specific ways have you tried to win your team's loyalty over the last month?

Just like in building loyalty in any relationship, remember that loyalty is not a one-way street. Start with building trust in the relationship with the many examples we have discussed throughout the book: being a leader who communicates

(continued)

(*continued*)

openly and honestly, being present and showing support for your teams, creating and respecting boundaries, and more. Once you have the foundation of trust, you can work on cultivating loyalty by showing up consistently, celebrating and acknowledging the efforts of your team, being trustworthy, and coaching them through mistakes.

Don't pull the "well, I'm the boss" card to demand loyalty from your team. When you don't demand loyalty like bad bosses do, and you lead effectively, that's when we gain loyalty as good leaders.

Many of us are leading using an old definition of what we expect loyalty to look like in our workplaces. Here are three ways we can stop ourselves and others from becoming the bad boss who demands loyalty at all costs.

Stop Hoarding Talent

A mentor once told me that my former bad boss Tony wouldn't let me leave his team because I had become indispensable. Tony relied on me to do things that were well outside of my job description. I happily obliged, thinking that doing more work would get me promoted and off his team. But Tony never had any intention of letting me go because I had become too valuable to him. He didn't want any other leader to have access to my experience and talents.

If we strive to be great leaders, we have to stop hoarding talent. I have watched many an HR team help with processes and tools for succession planning, career pathing, and setting clear expiration dates for time in role. And yet, bad bosses ignore these processes and aren't held accountable. They want to hold onto "the great talent." They don't consider the other talent out there who also has the potential to become great with onboarding, coaching, and support. They will make a myriad of excuses for hoarding talent and sometimes flat out lie:

- "Mita isn't ready yet. She has more to accomplish on my team."
- "Oh, I have spoken to Mita, and she's perfectly content in her role. She has no interest in moving teams right now."
- "I just had one person resign, and another person go on parental leave. Mita needs to stay to keep the ship afloat."

Consider the following to challenge the hoarding of talent by other leads (adjusting depending on the context and situation):

- "Mita has been in this role close to three years now. What are next steps for her?"
- "We agreed as a team on a process for rotating talent, giving them exposure to other parts of the business. If we don't let Mita rotate with everyone else, is that fair to her?"
- "When's the last time we had a conversation with Mita on what she wants next in her career?"

Our number-one job as leaders is to create more leaders. This means helping people move on to what they are meant to do next, helping them grow and advance their careers.

Be Honest and Upfront About Career Opportunities

According to one workplace study, a lack of professional growth opportunities is one of the top reasons employees leave companies.[6] In fact, 46% of employees said they left their last organization because they saw no opportunities to move on from their current role. Most employees want career advancement opportunities;

they don't want to stay in the same position for years on end just to demonstrate loyalty. Being able to work in different positions, rotate around divisions, and get promotions is all key as some aspire to work in higher positions. And a bad boss demanding loyalty and keeping them on their teams longer than they should could be the trigger for individuals to leave the company.

In my case, Tony had told me I would be in this role for 12 months. If something had changed with that timeline, he never let me know. He grew incensed when he found out I was asking other leaders for career advice.

Here's what differentiates bad bosses from good leaders when it comes to winning your team's loyalty: being honest and upfront about career opportunities. Consider the following to communicate (adjusting depending on the context and situation):

- "I know I said this would be a one-year assignment. Given the exciting initiative you are now leading, how would you feel about staying an additional year on the team? I think it would be a great experience for you to own this start to finish."
- "Unfortunately, all promotions are on hold for the rest of the year. We are committed to promoting you in January. What do you need from me in the interim to support you?"
- "If you join the team, you need to know this is a three-year assignment. I will be committed to coaching you and further developing your career."
- "I can't imagine how frustrated you must feel. I know you have been looking for an internal director role for several months. How can I help?"
- "Let's talk about development opportunities. Are there any courses you would be interested in taking? The company is offering a leadership course; I would like to nominate you to attend."

No one wants to feel like they are stuck in their career. Help them get unstuck by providing timely information on career opportunities and being open and honest about next steps.

When You Care About Someone's Career, Let Them Go

Finally, when we care about someone's career, we let them go. There's a lot of advice in the marketplace on how to resign, when to resign, what to say, and what not to do. And we don't talk enough about how leaders should show up in that moment when someone resigns to them.

This is not the time to question or demand their loyalty or guilt-trip them into staying. Show up with grace and kindness. Remember to congratulate them in the moment, don't delay announcing the news to the team, be considerate on the transition workload, and celebrate them. Follow up to have an exit interview to understand why they are leaving and what would have to change for them to stay. If they don't feel comfortable meeting with you, ask them to meet with HR so their thoughts can be shared with you in the future. There may be an opportunity to rehire or work with them again so how they offboard the company is just as important as how they onboarded.

Boomerang employees are on the rise. These individuals leave a company and then within a year or two return to the same company. According to one workplace study, 43% of individuals who quit their jobs during the pandemic now admit they were better off with their former employer; 20% of those individuals returned to their former job. For those who haven't boomeranged back, 41% would consider returning if it was presented as an option.[7] And according to a LinkedIn poll, 55% of leaders surveyed have hired a boomerang employee and would do it again; 26% of leaders say they haven't but would be open to hiring them.[8]

Bad bosses think they own their team members' careers and demand loyalty when it has not yet been earned. Good leaders understand that loyalty in the workplace is now something that we must earn and win over time. They do many of the things we have already discussed in the book, including creating a positive environment free from bullying, trusting their team's expertise and letting them make decisions and own their work, and finally offering opportunities for learning and career advancement. Overall, these good leaders make sure their team members feel they are engaged, their contributions matter, and that they are in charge of their own careers. Loyalty isn't guaranteed and it's certainly not built overnight. Don't let bad bosses like Tony Soprano convince you otherwise.

Tip for Leaders for Gaining Loyalty from Their Teams

- Start by asking yourself, do you demand loyalty, or do you try to earn loyalty?
- Remember three ways we can stop ourselves and others from becoming the bad boss who demands loyalty at all costs:
  - Stop hoarding talent.
  - Be honest and upfront about career opportunities.
  - When you care about someone's career, let them go.
- Loyalty in the workplace is now something that we must earn and win over time.

13

The Boss Who Was Grieving and Couldn't Show Up for Her Team

It is easier to share the stories of all the bad bosses I have worked for over the years.

It is much harder to admit that I have also been one of those bad bosses.

Valentine's Day 2017 was one of the most devastating days of my life. Without any warning, without any signs, without any notice, my father passed away. All these years later, I recall every detail of my mother's frantic call to tell me when she couldn't find my dad. I remember scrambling to the car with my husband and our two-year-old daughter and four-year-old son, the long drive from New York to Massachusetts, stuck in traffic, my daughter repeatedly vomiting all over me, then walking up the garage stairs into the house very late in the evening, praying that my father would be alive at home waiting for us. He was not.

The days that followed seemed like a nightmare we could not wake up from. While my parents' finances were fortunately in good order, my brother and I had a long list of to-dos: choosing a casket, arranging the cremation, selecting a burial suit for my dad, declining or accepting an autopsy, canceling my dad's cell phone and his Social Security benefits, transferring bills into my mom's name, writing an obituary. Then there was the task of telling family and friends, a lifetime's worth, knowing that with every conversation, we were reexperiencing the trauma of his death.

I had my husband call my boss's assistant to let my company know I would be out.

At the time, the company I worked for offered three days off for bereavement leave. I was able to take three weeks of paid time off with my team supporting me. Unfortunately, I know this is not everyone's experience.

"You look awful," my boss said as I entered his office.

"How did he die? Was it a heart attack? Do you know when he died? Did you do an autopsy?"

I was back at work, trying to stay busy, trying to find some sense of a "new normal," trying to start this next chapter of my life without my dad in it. And in my very first interaction with my boss, he inundated me with questions. He wouldn't stop asking me how my dad had died, wanting all the details.

I didn't want to answer any of his questions. And yet because I felt so exhausted by the grief I was experiencing, I relented. I sat there addressing his questions one by one. And as I provided those answers, I was reexperiencing the trauma of my dad's death.

Back at work, I found some colleagues avoiding me in the hallways like I was contagious with the flu. Others sent me quick emails, texts, and cards saying they were sorry for my loss. And a handful of colleagues who had also lost a loved one embraced me and checked in on me.

A few weeks after being back at work, my boss looked at me one afternoon and said, "Finally! You seem like you have your mojo back!" I looked at him, quickly slapping on a fake smile. The world continued on without my dad in it and so the expectation was clear: get over his death and get back to my old self.

After my dad's death, I found myself reverting back to old behaviors I had tried so hard to outgrow as a leader. I struggled with confidence during my early career, but over time I had grown bolder, well-respected, and accomplished. With the loss of my father, a stable and constant force in my life, I felt my decades of experience and confidence slipping away.

Now, I had trouble speaking up in meetings and sharing my point of view. I went to sit in the back of the room whenever I could. I started isolating myself from my team and colleagues. I suddenly doubted myself in every email exchange, every casual interaction, every meeting. I became incredibly sensitive to any kind of feedback, even if it was helpful coaching on how to make a recommendation stronger or a request to push a deadline out because the work was no longer urgent. I would lash out temporarily at individuals or run into the women's bathroom to collapse into a pile of tears.

With my dad no longer in the world, everything seemed uncertain, even at work.

On a number of occasions, I would cancel our weekly team meeting an hour before they were to start. I was supposed to be leading them. I had trouble focusing, wasn't sure what I would say to the team, or what value I would add. So I thought better to give people the time back or have one of the senior managers run the meeting. Sometimes I would give a reason for canceling; other times I didn't. I just canceled.

One afternoon, I shouted loudly at the security guard because I had left my badge in the other building and she wouldn't let me in. I was with some of my team members and rushing to get into the building to set up a meeting with the CEO. I left my badge in the other building. My team members watched me shout at her twice. I relented and went back and got my badge, rushed into the building and to the meeting. Two days later, I went back and found the security guard to apologize to her. I discovered that she had recently lost her mother.

I began emailing my team and colleagues late at night. Sometimes well past midnight, because I just couldn't sleep. I had recurring nightmares of my dad dying. I would send my team notes sometimes at 2 a.m. or 3 a.m. If I couldn't sleep, I thought I might as well be productive. I justified sending these emails because they were never urgent requests. I figured they could just read them in the morning. For years, I had shared stories about my terrible experience working for the Devil. Then quickly, and quietly, I had become the very boss, that very villain, I couldn't stand: the Devil who emails at midnight.

I fluctuated between being absent and then being overly present and micromanaging details that didn't matter. On some initiatives, I made no decisions and let my team decide what they wanted to do. On other initiatives, I got caught up on one detail that would hold up a decision for days. I questioned whether it was the right decision with my confidence shaken.

On another afternoon, a few hours before a presentation we were giving, I was annoyed with my team.

"I never got a chance to review the deck," I lamented at one of my team members' desks. "The meeting is in 90 minutes."

"Well . . . umm . . . we sent it to you a few times, we didn't hear back . . ." one of the women on my team stammered. "It should be in your inbox."

"No, I never saw a deck," I snapped back. I took out my phone and started scrolling. If there was a deck, I know I would have seen it.

And there it was. The deck. Not once. But twice. Nope, three times in my inbox. They had emailed it. And I hadn't responded. I pulled the deck up on my laptop, and over the next 60 minutes, they sat there and watched me change most of the deck. Then I sat in the meeting quietly in the back not saying a word, making them present mostly new slides they hadn't rehearsed before.

Finally, later that summer, one of my team members resigned. Months earlier, she had once grabbed me for tea and asked, "Are you doing okay? The team would love more time with you. We don't see you much anymore . . ."

"Well, I am here, I am around, just busy that's all," I had replied, completely annoyed. "That's what bosses do, we're busy leading," I said sarcastically.

"Okay, sure," she said uncomfortably. "I have to go now to a meeting. Bye." She walked off, and about five months later, gave me her two weeks' notice.

I held my breath when I looked over the exit interview notes human resources (HR) sent me after she left. That over the last several months, I wasn't present or involved with the team as I once had been. I had stopped coaching and teaching. She didn't see any career development or growth opportunities here anymore. She said she wished me all the best and I had once been one of the best bosses she had ever worked for.

I cried that night as I was driving home from work thinking about my dad. I cried because I thought of this team member and how I had let her and my team down. I cried because I had not given myself permission to grieve my dad. I had buried the grief, feeling the pressure to get over it quickly at work. I tried to distract myself with a mixture of junk food, online shopping, some days binging Netflix in the evening. And, of course, trying to raise my kids and be there for them, because they still needed diapers changed, wanted an endless supply of goldfish snacks, and required crazy hats and mismatched socks for their school spirit weeks. I also stayed focused on what I could to support my mom, who was on her journey of grieving.

By not dealing with my grief, I not only showed up as the Devil at work but also started to embody a number of my other bad bosses. While I wasn't napping at work, I went back and forth between being disengaged like the Napper to micromanaging like the Chopper. And while I didn't throw any Chanel shoes at anyone like Medusa, I did lose my temper on more than one occasion.

It was one of the more painful moments in my career, and more important, one of the most painful moments in my life. And yet, that wasn't an excuse for how badly I showed up at work and how unkindly I treated others around me.

In the months after my dad's death, I discovered one of his handkerchiefs in his study. For as long as I could remember, he kept one of these tucked in his pocket. It was his version of a small luxury—like a consistent gift to himself, despite what the world gave or took from him. He was an Indian immigrant engineer who left his family behind in Kolkata to start a life in the United States. He didn't have a community of support to fall back on. He struggled to fit into Corporate America. But despite all that, he became an executive of a Fortune 500 company.

As I slowly gave myself permission to grieve, I carried his handkerchief wherever I went. It reminded me what to do as I'd watched him do—to establish routines at work, to focus my attention. To practice self-care, I started taking long walks and made sure to eat lunch every day. I let the tears flow when they came and grieved. I built new connections with colleagues, took on new projects, began coleading our women's employee resource group, and helped my employer rethink its bereavement policies. I reached out to any colleague who had recently lost a loved one, regardless of whether I knew them or not. I wanted them to know they weren't alone in their grief at work.

Giving myself permission to heal helped me reclaim my voice and rebuild my confidence again as a leader. I crawled out of my bad boss phase. And it was a reminder that we can easily point out the bad bosses in our careers. It's always harder to look in the mirror and come to terms with the bad boss staring back at you.

★★★★★

We will all lose someone we love. We will all grieve. And yet, we still find it so painful, so uncomfortable, so difficult to talk about. And in our workplaces, we can act like grief doesn't even exist. Or rather, we don't want to make any room for it.

I've heard leaders make a variety of insensitive comments when it comes to team members grieving the loss of a loved one both behind closed doors and in front of an audience:

> "Where's the funeral? Why does she need a week off? I need her back in the office."

> "Who died? His grandfather? How old was he? We have a customer presentation that week."

> "My condolences to him. Getting back to work is the best way to get on with life."

> "Okay, I know he's on bereavement leave. But someone needs to call him—the customer needs a response."

> "Three weeks is an incredibly generous bereavement leave policy. How about five days instead?"

When we don't give individuals the time to grieve and heal, we are inviting them to bottle up their emotions and lock them away. To pretend everything is normal and just get back to work. And when we lead teams, and we aren't given the space or encouraged to grieve, there can be severe consequences. As someone who was carrying the heavy load of grief, I was disengaged, I wasn't present, and I struggled with my confidence and abilities to do my job. Not dealing with grief led me to embrace a number of bad boss behaviors. The very same behaviors I once had tried to and survived over the years. I wasn't able to be the good leader my team deserved.

Studies show that "the decreased productivity and increased absenteeism caused by grief costs the country over $75 billion per year."[1] Grief can also take on many forms, including divorce, battling an illness, ending of a relationship, injury, moving, a family member losing their job, wars and communities being under attack, or surviving a global pandemic as many of us did. And we know that grief is a long journey. Long after the funeral is over, we still grieve. Just as my former boss thought I was getting it together and had "my mojo back," I was falling apart inside.

While many organizations are rushing to rethink parental leave policies and wellness benefits, offer sabbatical leaves, and offer fancy perks to get teams back into the office five days a week, bereavement policies probably haven't been at the top of many lists. How can organizations better help grieving leaders and team members? Here are five things to keep in mind:

Give More Time Off

According to research conducted by the Society for Human Resource Management, 88% of businesses offer paid bereavement leave.[2] However, these periods typically extend from three days to the more generous five.[3] There are no federal laws requiring employers to provide workers with paid or unpaid time off following the death of a loved one. Oregon became one of the first states to require bereavement leave, thanks to legislation passed in 2014.[4]

Given all the tasks associated with arranging and/or traveling to a funeral, sorting out finances, and mourning one's loss, a few days off from the demands of our jobs doesn't cut it. Settling the affairs of those who those have passed away can take an average of 540 hours.[5] Organizations need to step up with more paid leave. Facebook set the bar in 2017 when it doubled its bereavement leave to 20 days paid following the loss of an immediate family member and up to 10 for an extended family member. Not coincidentally, former Facebook COO Sheryl Sandberg lost her husband in 2015 and wrote a book, *Option B*, about the experience.[6]

Remember, too, that bereavement, or grief, comes in several stages. So people might want to take time off intermittently as they need it, maybe 10 days now and 10 days later for a belated memorial service or trip, or to celebrate a date important to remember the person lost. Grief can continue to show up when you least expect it.

Expand the Definition of Family

Many bereavement leave policies distinguish between immediate and extended family members. The best are flexible, covering the loss of any loved one, including a partner, child, parent, grandparents, aunts and uncles, cousins, friends, and neighbors. Remember that loss comes in many forms, and we define who is part of our family in many different ways.

Miscarriage should also be included. Some companies, like Uber and Reddit, have taken this step.[7] According to the *Journal of Obstetrics and Gynecology*, 29% of women experience PSTD, 24% experience anxiety, and 11% experience moderate to severe depression after a miscarriage.[8] Bereavement leave is an opportunity for organizations to support people through all types of loss.

Don't Ask for Proof of Death

Do not ask to see a death certificate, obituary, or letter from a funeral home or hospital. This is uncomfortable, unnecessary, and assumes ill intent of someone asking for leave. The chances that someone would lie about the death of a loved one to abuse their company's bereavement leave policy are very small. Please don't use this as a moment to create mistrust and conflict with your employees. Believe employees when they say they are grieving and give them the space and time they need.

Offer Grief Counseling

Many organizations already provide some type of mental health support to their employees, and this is the time to remind people that it's available. Employee Assistance Programs (EAPs) are designed to help people through issues that might affect their performance at work and ultimately their well-being, and most EAPs include some form of assessments and counseling. Some organizations also provide subsidies for grief counselors whom employees choose on their own. I wish this was something I had access to at the time I had lost my father. Modern Health is another incredible partner, a platform for innovative companies that value the emotional well-being of their workforce. If your company isn't offering these benefits, encourage HR to consider it.

Take the Individual's Lead

When I came back to work after my dad died, I wanted to throw myself into existing projects and new initiatives. I needed to feel useful and find a new normal for what life after dad would look like. Other people might need less work, a slower pace, or different tasks, even after they've returned from leave. Please don't make decisions for those grieving. If they want to take on more work, give it to them. If they don't want to take their full bereavement time off, don't insist that they do. If they want to talk about the loss, listen. If they don't, respect their wishes. And if they need time to recover, support them.

It shouldn't be so hard to create a work environment where we are able to care for ourselves and care for each other. How we choose to show up for each other during the most painful and traumatic periods of our lives is something we will remember; it stays with us. And when we expect individuals who are leading teams to stay strong and show up with a brave face, despite the circumstances, it only creates the perfect recipe for creating another bad boss. We can all become "that bad boss" depending on the environment and the challenges we are facing not only at the conference room table but also in what we are grappling with at our kitchen tables, in our homes, and in our communities. When we give ourselves permission to grieve as leaders, we role model that for others as well on our teams. We can show up as the good leaders our teams deserve.

How Can We Support Colleagues Who Are Grieving the Loss of a Loved One?

One of the biggest mistakes we make when trying to support team members who just lost someone they love is what my former boss did: asking them how the person died. No matter how curious you are, this is not the time to become an investigative journalist. There's no reason to follow the "I'm so sorry for your loss" with "How did he die?"

If we want to genuinely support a team member who is grieving the loss of a loved one, let's move on from our

(continued)

(*continued*)

curiosity of how they passed away. When and if a coworker is ready to share how they lost their loved one, they will share with you. Instead, start by focusing on these three ways to help support their grieving journey.

Give Them The Time They Need

Even if your company's bereavement leave policy doesn't allow for much time off, as a leader, you can do the right thing and give extra time to your grieving team member. You don't need an employee handbook to tell you to do the right thing in an employee's time of need. And as a fellow team member, you can offer to cover projects, attend meetings, and stay on track for deadlines on their behalf. Remember that grief can be cruel and show up days and months later. Support team members in taking days off to focus on their well-being and their grieving journey.

Show Up with Support

I remember a friend losing a parent, and his boss kept texting him nonstop, asking him what sorts of meals his family liked. "Do you eat pasta?" The next day after her text went unanswered, "Do you like pizza? Are you vegetarian?" And finally, "I was trying to be helpful and send some meals, but I haven't heard back. Should I just send a fruit basket instead?" My friend felt overwhelmed by the texts, then felt guilty. Because amid dealing with funeral arrangements and hosting family members, he felt pressured to respond to the boss's texts regarding his family's food preferences.

Sometimes, we just need to show up with support when someone is grieving. Don't continue to reach out to the person grieving, asking for a response. They probably received your message and aren't able to respond to you yet for a variety of reasons. Give them the space to respond when they are ready.

If you do want to send meals, ask others if they know of any dietary restrictions. When in doubt send a Door-Dash or Uber Eats gift card, or a gift card to a local restaurant. You can offer to watch someone's children, walk their dog, have coffee and bagels delivered to their home, send flowers to the funeral home, or send a card. Whatever support you show will be appreciated and remembered, even if they don't take you up on your offer to help.

Continue to Check In

Several weeks after my father died, I was back at work in an all-day leadership off-site. I remember staring out the window at the bright blue sky. The beautiful blue color reminded me of a beautiful Indian kurta my dad used to always wear. I ran to the bathroom and burst into tears. As I exited the ladies' room, one of the men I worked with said to me, "Oh, that upset that our budgets are getting cut?" He laughed and walked away.

Another colleague ran over and knew exactly what was wrong. She squeezed my arm in support and walked with me to get a coffee. We walked in silence as she offered me a tissue. We got our coffee and sipped in silence. She asked me if she could do anything for me that day. I said I would like to leave the meeting early. She said she would let our boss know and pass along any notes she took.

Don't forget to check in with colleagues. After my dad died, some colleagues offered condolences and then avoided me in the hallways, not knowing what else to say. And in retrospect, I don't blame them. We don't talk enough about

(continued)

(*continued*)

grief in our workplaces or in our communities. When we lose someone we love, we are just at the beginning of our journey to heal, honor, and remember them. Continue to check in with colleagues on how you can help support them, even as the weeks and months pass.

As time went by, I appreciated sharing stories about my dad and what a great inspiration he will always be to me. I still to this day have former coworkers who remember the date that my dad died and text me to say they are thinking of me. Remember, there's no expiration on grief. It's all of our jobs to show up for each other in our greatest time of need.

Tips on How to Make Space for Grief at Work

- Here are five ways organizations can help leaders and the team members grieve:
  - Give more time off.
  - Expand the definition of family.
  - Don't ask for proof of death.
  - Offer grief counseling.
  - Take the individual's lead.
- How can we support colleagues who are grieving the loss of a loved one?
  - Give them the time they need.
  - Show up with support.
  - Continue to check in.
- Remember, how we choose to show up for each other during the most painful and traumatic periods of our lives is something we will remember and that stays with us.

Conclusion

I have always said that every bad boss I experienced made me stronger. Surviving bad bosses like the Devil, the Sheriff, the Napper, the Chopper, the White Rabbit, Medusa, the Great Pretender, the Grinner, the Cheerleader, Gossip Girl, Spotlight, and Tony has made me be a better leader and a better person. When I couldn't show up for my team when I was grieving, it was an incredibly humbling moment to recognize that small and big life-altering events can unexpectedly send us spiraling into bad boss territory.

Every bad boss behavior I encountered continues to serve as a reminder on **how not to lead** in the workplace. But it doesn't have to be that way.

I wrote this book because so much of what's available in the marketplace when it comes to bad bosses focuses on how to survive, outwit, make it through, endure, outlast, withstand, and navigate working for a bad boss. Because it's easier to excuse, dismiss, minimize, overlook, or flat out deny bad boss behavior. It's easier to tell everyone else, the individuals usually with less power or authority in our organizations, to grin and bear the bad boss and provide them with a laundry list of ways to survive this moment in their careers. But the real work, the hard work, the meaningful work is when each of us looks in the mirror and realizes that the bad boss isn't some Disney or Marvel villain. That at any given point in time in our careers, each and every one of us has the potential and can become the Devil who emails at midnight.

There aren't enough words, space, or time to cover every single bad boss behavior we may have experienced in our workplaces. My hope is that this book sparks more dialogue for you and your teams on behaviors you will no longer tolerate and behaviors you will work on changing together. And it reminds you of the power and responsibility we have to build more inclusive and healthy workplaces where everyone has an opportunity to thrive.

I hope you will come back to this book as a reference, share it with other leaders and colleagues, and that this book also serves as a reminder that leadership is not a right. It's not something you are owed or guaranteed or that you automatically deserve. Leadership is an honor, leadership is fragile, leadership is humbling. Leading others is a privilege. To help someone else become a leader is a responsibility we all must take much more seriously.

Over the course of my career, I have had a lot of bad bosses hurt me, chip away at me, and take away my voice. And I have had a number of good leaders help heal me. And help me find my voice again.

Imagine a world of work where we didn't need good leaders to help heal us. A world of work where good leaders simply just outnumbered the bad bosses. A world of work where we didn't allow bad boss behaviors to survive or in some cases thrive, infecting others, and where bad bosses eventually became extinct. A world of work where we all committed to being the good leader we needed, the good leader we never had.

So now, we can stop talking about bad bosses. And focus on striving to be that good leader we always wished we had worked for.

And when your team and your colleagues let you know that you are in fact a good leader, don't stop there.

Aspire to be great.

Notes

Introduction

1. Andrew Naber, "One Third of Your Life Is Spent at Work," n.d., https://www.gettysburg.edu/news/stories?id=79db7b 34-630c-4f49-ad32-4ab9ea48e72b.

Chapter 2

1. HR Acuity, "2023 Workplace Harassment & Employee Misconduct Insights," 2023, https://www.hracuity.com/ resources/research/workplace-harassment-and-employee-misconduct-insights.
2. Workplace Bullying Institute, "2021 WBI U.S. Workplace Bullying Survey," 2021, https://workplacebullying.org/ 2021-wbi-survey-infographic.
3. Ella F. Washington, "Recognizing and Responding to Micro-aggressions at Work," *Harvard Business Review*, May 10, 2022, https://hbr.org/2022/05/recognizing-and-responding-to-microaggressions-at-work.
4. S. McFeely and B. Wigert, "This Fixable Problem Costs U.S. Businesses $1 Trillion," Gallup Workplace, March 13, 2019, https://www.gallup.com/workplace/247391/fixable-problem-costs-businesses-trillion.aspx.

5. T. DeAngelis, "Unmasking 'Racial Micro Aggressions,'" *Monitor on Psychology* 40, no. 2 (2009): 42, https://www.apa.org/monitor/2009/02/microaggression.

6. DeAngelis, "Unmasking 'Racial Micro Aggressions,'" 42.

7. K. Thompson, "Antiracism's Ibram Kendi Thinks Big: Why Not Equality Right Now? *USA Today*, February 4, 2021, https://www.usatoday.com/story/news/2021/02/02/black-history-month-antiracism-ibram-kendi/6568208002.

8. Ruchika T. Malhotra, "We Need to Retire the Term 'Micro-aggressions,'" *Harvard Business Review*, March 8, 2022, https://hbr.org/2022/03/we-need-to-retire-the-term-microaggressions#.

9. C. Coleman, "The Culture of Any Organization Is Shaped by the Worst Behavior the Leader Is Willing to Tolerate," Culture Wise, January 11, 2022, https://blog.culturewise.com/the-culture-of-any-organization-is-shaped-by-the-worst-behavior-the-leader-is-willing-to-tolerate.

Chapter 3

1. R. Pendell, "Employee Engagement Strategies: Fixing the World's $8.8 Trillion Problem," 2023, https://www.gallup.com/workplace/393497/world-trillion-workplace-problem.aspx.

2. S. Adler, "The Corrosive Impact of Disengaging Leaders," 2021, https://www.thehrdirector.com/features/leadership/corrosive-impact-disengaging-leaders/.

3. L. Parsons, "How to Engage a Disengaged Employee," 2022, https://professional.dce.harvard.edu/blog/how-to-engage-a-disengaged-employee/.

4. K. Ferry, "Sleeping on the Job, Literally," 2024, https://www.kornferry.com/insights/this-week-in-leadership/sleeping-on-the-job-literally.

Chapter 4

1. S. Kesteven, Z. Ferguson, and L. Leong, "Do You Have a Micromanaging Boss? Here's How to Work with Them," n.d., https://www.msn.com/en-au/news/other/do-you-have-a-micromanaging-boss-here-s-how-to-work-with-them/ar-BB1qUokc.
2. Monster, "Poll Results: Workplace Red Flags," n.d., https://learnmore.monster.com/workplace-red-flags-poll-results.
3. L. Kalser, "Micromanaging Bosses Are a Workplace Red Flag, Workers Say," 2023, https://www.hrdive.com/news/micromanaging-bosses-workplace-red-flag/692667/.
4. B. Gentry, "Developing New Managers? How to Set Your First-Time Leaders Up for Success," 2022, https://www.ccl.org/articles/leading-effectively-articles/prepare-first-time-leaders-success/.
5. Training Industry, "Learning Services and Outsourcing: The Size of the Training Industry," n.d., https://trainingindustry.com/wiki/learning-services-and-outsourcing/size-of-training-industry/.

Chapter 5

1. Disney, "The Most Quotable Sayings from *Alice in Wonderland*," n.d., https://news.disney.com/alice-in-wonderland-quotes.
2. Hubspot for Startups logo for Startups, "11 Ways to Increase Startup Sales Productivity," n.d., https://www.hubspot.com/startups/maximizing-startup-sales-productivity#:~:text=According%20to%20research%2C%20lost%20productivity,and%20planning%2C%20and%20even%20burnout.

Chapter 6

1. C. Crist, "One-Third of Corporate Managers Lead with Fear, Survey Says," 2023, https://www.hrdive.com/news/fear-based-corporate-managers/699149/.
2. Ibid.
3. Ibid.
4. Ibid.
5. Ibid.
6. A. Bunker, "What Is NPS? The Ultimate Guide to Boosting your Net Promoter Score," n.d., https://www.qualtrics.com/experience-management/customer/net-promoter-score/.
7. World Health Organization, "Burn-Out an "Occupational Phenomenon": International Classification of Diseases," 2019, https://www.who.int/news/item/28-05-2019-burn-out-an-occupational-phenomenon-international-classification-of-diseases.
8. Ibid.
9. B. Wigert and S. Agrawal, "Employee Burnout, Part 1: The 5 Main Causes," 2018, https://www.gallup.com/workplace/237059/employee-burnout-part-main-causes.aspx#:~:text=Although%20burnout%20has%20become%20%22just,actively%20seeking%20a%20different%20job.
10. Mayo Clinic, "Job Burnout: How to Spot It and Take Action," n.d., https://www.mayoclinic.org/healthy-lifestyle/adult-health/in-depth/burnout/art-20046642.

Chapter 7

1. E. Samuels, "The Past, Present, and Future of Pregnancy in the Workplace," 2024, https://onlabor.org/the-past-present-and-future-of-pregnancy-in-the-workplace/.
2. Ibid.

3. T. Luhby, "Pregnant Workers and Nursing Moms Have New Protections on the Job," 2023, https://www.cnn.com/2023/06/27/politics/pregnant-workers-nursing-moms-jobs/index.html.

4. Samuels, "The Past, Present, and Future of Pregnancy in the Workplace."

5. Ibid.

6. N. Kitroeff and J. Silver-Greenberg, "Pregnancy Discrimination Is Rampant Inside America's Biggest Companies," 2019, https://www.nytimes.com/interactive/2018/06/15/business/pregnancy-discrimination.html.

7. Ibid.

8. S. Correll, S. Benard, and I. Paik, "Getting a Job: Is There a Motherhood Penalty?," 2007, https://gap.hks.harvard.edu/getting-job-there-motherhood-penalty.

9. Ibid.

10. Ibid.

11. World Economic Forum, "The Motherhood Penalty: How Childcare and Paternity Leave Can Reduce the Gender Pay Gap," 2022, https://www.weforum.org/stories/2022/05/reduce-motherhood-penalty-gender-pay-gap/.

12. National Women's Law Center, "The Wage Gap Robs Mothers of What They're Owed," 2024, https://nwlc.org/resource/mothers-wage-gap/.

13. Correll et al., "Getting a Job: Is There a Motherhood Penalty?"

14. Ibid.

15. M. Fox, "'The Motherhood Penalty' Is Real, and It Costs Women $16,000 a Year in Lost Wages," 2019, https://www.cnbc.com/2019/03/25/the-motherhood-penalty-costs-women-16000-a-year-in-lost-wages.html.

16. AAUW, "7 Things to Know About Pregnancy Discrimination," n.d., https://www.aauw.org/resources/legal/7-things-pregnancy-discrimination/.

17. U.S. Equal Employment Opportunity Commission, "Pregnancy Discrimination and Pregnancy-Related Disability Discrimination," n.d., https://www.eeoc.gov/pregnancy-discrimination.

18. National Women's Law Center, "Pregnant at Work? Know Your Rights," 2018, https://nwlc.org/resource/pregnant-at-work-know-your-rights/.

Chapter 8

1. Perceptyx, "Nearly a Quarter of All Employees Are Working for the Worst Manager They've Ever Had," 2023, https://blog.perceptyx.com/nearly-a-quarter-of-all-employees-are-working-for-the-worst-manager-theyve-ever-had.

2. Ibid.

3. Fast Company, "Toxic Workplaces Are Bad for Workers. They Are Also Bad for Business," 2024, https://www.fastcompany.com/91060915/toxic-workplaces-are-bad-for-workers-they-are-also-bad-for-business.

4. Carrier Management, "Incompetent Bosses: Study Says Responses to Them Vary by Age," 2023, https://www.carriermanagement.com/news/2023/06/13/249539.htm.

5. Fast Company, "Why Competent Workers Become Incompetent Managers," 2024, https://www.fastcompany.com/91170842/why-competent-workers-become-incompetent-managers.

6. Ibid.

7. Ibid.

8. C. DeSantis, "How to Be Your Own Greatest Champion," 2021, https://medium.com/@christydesantis/how-to-be-your-own-greatest-champion-8c6c14e3d64f.

9. J. Guynn and J. Fraser, "How Diverse Is Corporate America? There Are More Black Leaders but White Men Still Run It," 2023, https://www.usatoday.com/in-depth/money/2023/02/16/white-men-corporate-america-diversity/11114830002/.

10. Ibid.

11. A. Gugushvili and G. Bulczak, "Physical Attractiveness and Intergenerational Social Mobility," *Social Science Quarterly* 104, no. 7 (2023): 1360–82, https://onlinelibrary.wiley.com/doi/10.1111/ssqu.13320.

12. M. Smith, "Men Benefit More from Their Looks at Work Than Women Do, New Research Shows," 2024, https://www.cnbc.com/2024/02/02/men-benefit-more-from-their-looks-at-work-than-women-do-new-research-shows.html.

13. Ibid.

14. C. Canway, "What Does Poor Onboarding Really Do to Your Team," 2024, https://www.businessnewsdaily.com/9936-consequences-poor-onboarding.html.

15. Fast Company, "Why Competent Workers Become Incompetent Managers."

16. Ibid.

Chapter 9

1. J. Moss, "Creating a Happier Workplace Is Possible—and Worth It," 2023, https://hbr.org/2023/10/creating-a-happier-workplace-is-possible-and-worth-it.

2. University of Oxford, "Happy Workers Are 13% More Productive," 2019, https://www.ox.ac.uk/news/2019-10-24-happy-workers-are-13-more-productive.

3. Wharton Work, "Improve Productivity and Success with Five 'Positivity' Habits," 2014, https://executiveeducation.wharton.upenn.edu/thought-leadership/wharton-at-work/2014/03/positivity-habits/.

4. Great Place to Work, "BetterUp," 2022, https://www.greatplacetowork.com/certified-company/7005176.

5. E. Perry, "Improve Your Life with a New Outlook: 10 Benefits of Positive Thinking," 2022, https://www.betterup.com/blog/positive-thinking-benefits.

6. M. Schwantes, "A New Study Reveals That Telling Women They Need to Smile More Is Bad for Business. Here's Why," 2019, https://www.inc.com/marcel-schwantes/a-new-study-reveals-that-telling-women-they-need-to-smile-more-is-bad-for-business-heres-why.html.

7. D. Motro, Jonathan B. Evans, Aleksander P. J. Ellis, and L. Benson III, "The 'Angry Black Woman' Stereotype at Work," 2022, https://hbr.org/2022/01/the-angry-black-woman-stereotype-at-work.

8. Ibid.

9. A. Dorsey, "Seriously, Why Are Women Expected to Smile All the Time?," 2015, https://www.womenshealthmag.com/life/a19934710/women-expected-to-smile/.

Chapter 10

1. J. Warren, "UC Riverside Study Busts Myths About Gossip," 2019, https://news.ucr.edu/articles/2019/05/03/uc-riverside-study-busts-myths-about-gossip.

2. A. Aubrey, "We Gossip About 52 Minutes a Day. That May Not Be as Toxic as It Sounds," 2019, https://www.npr.org/sections/health-shots/2019/05/13/722141820/we-gossip-about-52-minutes-a-day-that-may-not-be-as-toxic-as-it-sounds.

3. A. Ossola, "The Psychology of Why We Love—and Need—to Gossip," 2022, https://www.thedailybeast.com/the-psychology-of-why-we-love-and-need-to-gossip/.

Chapter 11

1. https://www.businesswire.com/news/home/20191014005015/en/Boss-Professionals-Managers-Credit-Work-Korn-Ferry.

2. T. E. Holmes, T "Nearly Half of Workers Say Bosses Have Taken Credit for Their Work," 2019, https://finance.yahoo.com/news/nearly-half-workers-bosses-taken-175929075.html?guccounter=1.
3. Ibid.
4. H. S. Truman, "Truman Quotes," n.d., https://www.trumanlibraryinstitute.org/truman/truman-quotes/page/5/.

Chapter 12

1. HBO, "The Sopranos," n.d., https://www.hbo.com/the-sopranos.
2. C. Kolmar, "Average Number of Jobs in a Lifetime [2023]: How Many Jobs Does the Average Person Have," 2013, https://www.zippia.com/advice/average-number-jobs-in-lifetime/.
3. Ibid.
4. D. Wilkie, "Just Because Your Workers Feel Loyal Doesn't Mean They'll Stay," 2020, https://www.shrm.org/topics-tools/news/employee-relations/just-workers-feel-loyal-doesnt-mean-theyll-stay.
5. R. Wartzman, "The End of Loyalty," 2017, https://www.hachettebookgroup.com/titles/rick-wartzman/the-end-of-loyalty/9781586489151/?lens=publicaffairs.
6. Wilkie, "Just Because Your Workers Feel Loyal Doesn't Mean They'll Stay."
7. D. Locapo, "15+ Million Pandemic-Era U.S. Job Quitters Say They Were Better Off in Their Old Job," 2022, https://www.ukg.com/about-us/newsroom/15-million-pandemic-era-us-job-quitters-say-they-were-better-their-old-job.
8. https://www.reedglobal.us/blog/2023/07/boomerang-the-rise-in-returning-employees?source=google.com.

Chapter 13

1. ExtensisHR, "Is It Time to Rethink Your Bereavement Leave Policy?," 2025, https://extensishr.com/resource/blogs/bereavement-leave-policy/#:~:text=Not%20providing%20paid%20time%20off,an%20average%20of%20540%20hours.

2. K. Doheny, "COVID-19 Grief Is Different: What Managers Should Know," 2021, https://www.shrm.org/topics-tools/news/managing-smart/covid-19-grief-different-managers-know.

3. R. Mayhew, "The Average HR Policy for Time Off for Deaths in Family," n.d., https://smallbusiness.chron.com/average-hr-policy-time-off-deaths-family-68630.html.

4. Bullivant Houser, "Oregon Becomes First State to Mandate Protected Bereavement Leave," n.d., https://www.bullivant.com/oregon-becomes-first-state-to-mandate-protected-bereavement-leave/.

5. ExtensisHR, "Is It Time to Rethink Your Bereavement Leave Policy?"

6. B. Luscombe, "Life After Death," n.d., https://time.com/sheryl-sandberg-option-b/.

7. R. Dube, "Miscarriage at Work," 2020, https://www.today.com/parents/miscarriage-leave-new-frontier-parental-benefits-t173482.

8. S. Maitlis and G. Petriglieri, "Going Back to Work After a Pregnancy Loss," 2019, https://hbr.org/2019/12/going-back-to-work-after-a-pregnancy-loss.

Acknowledgments

I want to thank my mother, Manjula, who reminded me of specific details to include in these stories that I had long forgotten. She lived many of these bad boss moments with me. My brother, Sumit, who also patiently listened to me complain about my bad bosses over the years. My sister-in-law, Allison, for once again engaging our kids as I made final edits to this book. My husband, Piyush, who has always provided wise counsel when I was working for bad bosses, even though I wasn't always ready to hear it.

I imagine my father, who is no longer here with us, sitting in his red chair and sipping a cup of tea while reading this book. I wonder what bad boss stories he would have shared with me.

My children, Priya and Jay; my nieces Lily, Emma, and Julia; and my nephew, Zachary: I hope you work for more good leaders than bad bosses. And I hope those bad bosses you do work for remind you to always strive to be a better leader and a better human.

Thank you to my team of advisors for trusting my vision for this book: Josh Getzler, Jillian Schelzi, Julie Kerr, Victoria Savanh, Trinity Crompton, and Sarah Mason.

And thank you to my circle who has been cheering me on for this book: Christy DeSantis, Lan Phan, Asha Santos,

Diana Santiago, Danni Maggin, Nisha Thomas Dearborn, Charli Spellane, Madhura Phadke, Tracy Avin, Jill Katz, Josh Saterman, Sonali Pai, Pallavi Arora, Kevin Messam, LaQuanda Murray, Jahmaal Marshall, Cate Luzio, Dinah Alobeid, Daisy Lovelace, Rich Cardona, LaToya Rose, Chris Gee, and many more individuals who continue to support me on my journey. I am grateful for you all.

About the Author

Mita Mallick is a *Wall Street Journal* and *USA Today* best-selling author. She's on a mission to fix what's broken in our workplaces. She's a corporate changemaker with a track record of transforming businesses and has had an extensive career as a marketing and human resources executive. Mallick has brought her talent and expertise to companies like Unilever, Pfizer, AVON, Johnson & Johnson, Carta, and more. She's a highly sought-after speaker and business coach to startup founders, executives, and public company CEOs.

Mallick is a LinkedIn Top Voice and was named to the Thinkers50 Radar List. Mallick is a contributor for *Harvard Business Review*, *Fast Company*, *Time magazine*, *Entrepreneur*, and *Adweek* on a range of cultural, workplace, and marketing topics. She has been featured in the *New York Times*, *The Wall Street Journal*, the *Washington Post*, *Forbes*, *Axios*, *Essence*, *Cosmopolitan* magazine, and *Business Insider*. She was featured in a documentary created by Soledad O'Brien Productions for CBS News entitled *Women in the Workplace and the Unfinished Fight for Equality*. Mallick holds a BA from Barnard College, Columbia University, and an MBA from Duke University's Fuqua School of Business. She lives in New Jersey with her husband and two children.

Index

ALSO FROM
MITA
MALLICK

WALL STREET JOURNAL BESTSELLER

REIMAGINE
INCLUSION

DEBUNKING **13** MYTHS TO

TRANSFORM YOUR WORKPLACE

MITA MALLICK

WILEY

Reimagine Inclusion • ISBN: 978-1-394-17709-7

WILEY